TAKE ME
to the
KING

TAKE ME
to the
KING

All churched out…A call
for Kings to reclaim the Kingdom

JOEL C. WIGGINS

MILESTONE
PUBLISHING HOUSE

Scripture quotations marked (NIV) are taken from the Holy Bible, New International Version®, NIV®. Copyright © 1973, 1978, 1984, 2011 by Biblica, Inc.™ Used by permission of Zondervan. All rights reserved worldwide. www.zondervan.com. The "NIV" and "New International Version" are trademarks registered in the United States Patent and Trademark Office by Biblica, Inc.™ Scripture quotations marked "KJV" are taken from the Holy Bible, King James Version (Public Domain). Scripture quotations marked (AMP) are taken from the Amplified Bible, Copyright © 1954, 1958, 1962, 1964, 1965, 1987 by The Lockman Foundation. Used by permission. Scriptures Quotations marked "GNB" are from the Good News Bible © 1994 published by the Bible Societies/HarperCollins Publishers Ltd UK, Good News Bible © American Bible Society 1966, 1971, 1976, 1992. Used with permission. Scripture quotations marked "NASB" are taken from the New American Standard Bible®, Copyright © 1960, 1962, 1963, 1968, 1971, 1972, 1973, 1975, 1977, 1995 by The Lockman Foundation. Used by permission.

Take Me to the King: All churched out...A call for Kings to reclaim the Kingdom / by Joel C. Wiggins

ISBN: 978-0-9912013-8-8 (paperback)
ISBN: 978-0-9912013-8-9 (hardcover)

MILESTONE
PUBLISHING HOUSE

Published by Milestone Publishing
7413 Six Forks Road, Suite 301, Raleigh, NC 27615

Cover design by Roy Roper, wideyedesign.net
Original cover photos by Leonardo Patrizi and Jezperklauzen
Interior page design by the Ink Studio

Disclaimer:

Printed in the United States of America

DEDICATION

This book is dedicated first to the Lord Jesus, the King of my world, and to the Father for His grace and love. I dedicate this book to my wife, Katrina, and our family: to my son, Joshua, for being an up-and-coming King, and to my daughters, Christina and Reagan, for being Queens in the making.

This book is also dedicated to every misguided King who has lost his way: to the many young men who are sitting in a lost place such as gangs and prisons, who have never walked in their calling as Kings in the Marketplace. My heart is with you, as I think of the impact you could have on your families and in our communities if you receive the guidance that you so need from other Kings.

I also dedicate this work to the true apostles, prophets, teachers, pastors and evangelists who are equipping the saints for the work of the Kingdom.

CONTENTS

Contents

ACKNOWLEDGMENTS

First and foremost, I thank the Father for giving me the revelation that I will share through this work. I thank my wife, Katrina, for being by my side throughout our marriage and doing all she has done to make it possible for me to function as the Lord created me.

I thank my family for sharing me with this work. To my son, Joshua, I thank you for reminding me of how important it is to be the best father I can be. I am proud of you and look forward to you coming into your "kingship."

To my daughters, Christina and Reagan, you inspire me every day to be better and to leave the path of how a family and father should be well marked for you to follow.

To my mother, Verna, who helped me become the person I am today. I thank you and love you.

I thank my mentors, Fred Beans and Larry Titus, who first taught me the power of a true discipleship model.

Thank you also to Ericka D. Jackson, Ericka Balcom and Diana Summers for assisting me in putting this work together.

INTRODUCTION

The Purpose of this Book

This book was born out of a love for God, His Kingdom and the Body of Christ. It was birthed out of a grieving I experienced in seeing the natural order of the Kingdom and the roles of the five-fold ministry distorted in many worship centers and operating out of what I believe to be God's order. Through this shared revelation knowledge, it is my desire that the body and Kingdom will function as ordained, with all gifts, ministries and anointing fulfilling their assigned roles and working in harmony to build His Kingdom and stronger communities.

My intent is to lift up the name of Jesus Christ and our loving Father and to expose the process that prevents the manifestation of the Kingdom in our daily lives. I challenge the tradition that we hold so dear, which causes us to not question the results in our daily lives. When I look at the Black Christian community, I see results that reflect bondage and demonic influence. I've learned that no matter how great the city is for the quality of life of its citizens, the Christian Black community experiences far different results. I challenge a model that resembles slavery in far too many ways, along with the results. I challenge the minds and hearts of a people who have been taught to spend most of their time in a worship center, but not being a light in their community.

How did I get here? The first seed was planted in my up-close encounters with a good number of the pastors in my community. Once I became involved in the clothing business, I interacted on a regular basis with pastors. I wondered why God was putting me around so many of them, so frequently. In some of my other businesses, many pastors became returning customers, and they showed me a consistent pattern to which I had not been exposed before.

Part of this pattern included them almost always asking for a discount and to be given some things for free. The thought was that my giving them free or discounted services was like giving it to God. The other pattern was that they bragged a great deal about their perceived influence over the hearts and minds of the community. This does not happen in the realm of highly successful business owners, and it left me perplexed. I did not understand many of these pastors, who seemed to believe that the whole world revolved around them. This interaction was disturbing to me and, honestly, there were times when I pleaded with God to remove me from being around them.

What many of my fellow businessmen from different cultures had been telling me was right—far too many Black pastors were not contributing to real change in their communities. Although I didn't want to believe these businessmen, their assessment proved to be undeniable. Just like a hustler, the mindset of too many pastors was to take advantage of my business by asking me to give them a deeply discounted deal and, in exchange, they would connect me with all of these other pastors. Most of them were trying to impress one another, and very few of them truly understood or respected the operations of the marketplace. Almost all of them sounded the same. They often portrayed themselves as the gatekeepers for their community and the key to any possible success within their community. It was as if they were saying, "We are the Kings who control everything that happens in our community. We are the only voice to influence the people."

I would try to support their ministries by writing checks or by just attending some of their events, but I found this to be quite unsettling. I noticed that very little work was being done for the Kingdom, while a great deal of work was being done to grow their names and ministries. The teaching focused on prosperity and serving the worship center services. The pastors were intent on enriching themselves and their worship centers. If the sermon was not about how to acquire material possessions, then it was about honoring the pastor and bolstering his powerful status in the community. Above all, the pastors appealed for money. They even made their requests for money by playing videos of themselves boarding airplanes. Pastors' anniversaries were celebrated with people standing in line, announcing how much money they were giving to express their "gratitude" to the pastor.

This politically and financially-focused culture was driven by a mindset of fear. These pastors spoke the language of an upper slave whose master had commissioned him to control the lower slaves, but who never truly knew how to shepherd.

After years of closely observing this common behavior, coupled with my upbringing around the state of communities led by pastors, I recognized the underlying dynamics that explained the huge discrepancy between pastors and businessmen.

I believe the gifts placed inside the other members of the body of Christ must be assessed and released to help equip others on how to live. I strongly believe that God, our Creator, has placed many talents and gifts in my people that have sat dormant for so many years. The setup that makes pastors the head of our community is not seen in any other community of believers in our country. Where did this model originate and why is it still present?

Where Does A King Fit In The Body of Christ?

As I progressed further in my walk with the Lord, I understood that in the Bible, the Kings were the businessmen, and their responsibility was to partner with the priest in their role as leaders in building the community and teaching others to do the same. They had a distinctly different role from that of the priests or pastors. The distinction between these roles will be further explained.

These roles became increasingly evident the more pastors I had as clients in my businesses. I often received invitations to their churches and events. What commonly happened to me while attending these events was they would offer me the best parking spaces, the front row seats, or they would publicly acknowledge me. All of these behaviors are what a true King or businessman despises. Why would a King, who is used to being approached and catered to for access to his resources, want this from a worship center? This is the place where he comes for the sole purpose of being fed the Word. I wonder if they had ever read James 2:1-4 (NIV) which states:

> *"My brothers and sisters, believers in our glorious Lord Jesus Christ must not show favoritism. Suppose a man comes into your meeting wearing a gold ring and fine clothes, and a poor man in filthy old clothes also comes in. If you show special attention to the man wearing fine clothes and say, "Here's a good seat for you," but say to the poor man, "You stand there" or "Sit on the floor by my feet," have you not discriminated among yourselves and become judges with evil thoughts?"*

I later came to understand the reason why they gave me this preferential treatment. They thought that this was what I wanted, and if they kept me happy, I would give more money to their ministries. In other words, they assumed that I was like them. This could not have been further from the truth.

Jesus speaks to the nature of those who like their seats in the marketplace and special treatment. He describes it this way when the scribes and Pharisees sat in Moses' seat for the purpose of drawing attention to themselves:

> *The scribes and the Pharisees sit in Moses' seat. Therefore whatever they tell you to observe, that observe and do, but do not do according to their works; for they say, and do not do. For they bind heavy burdens, hard to bear, and lay them on men's shoulders; but they themselves will not move them with one of their fingers. But all their works they do to be seen by men. They make their phylacteries broad and enlarge the borders of their garments. They love the best places at feasts, the best seats in the synagogues, greetings in the marketplaces, and to be called by men, "Rabbi, Rabbi." But you, do not be called "Rabbi"; for One is your Teacher, the Christ, and you are all brethren.* (Matthew 23:2–8, NIV)

This scripture continues in verses 11–13 to say:

But he who is greatest among you shall be your servant. And whoever exalts himself will be humbled, and he who humbles himself will be exalted. But woe to you, scribes and Pharisees, hypocrites! (Matthew 23:11-13, NIV)

The priests wanted Jesus killed, and the accusation was that He claimed to be the King of the Jews. The priests feared that they would be subject to a King. The King came to free the people from bondage and make God visible, just as a righteous King would do today.

I was often invited to a pastor's office. Their conversation usually went something like this. "Doc, did you see how state-of-the-art this facility is?" *or* "Did you see the magnificent family life center I built?" This comment or something close to it was then followed by, "Let me show you my building plans." They would then show me the buildings they had already built or were in the process of building. Next they would talk about or show me the books they had written, where they lived, or how many people attended their church. My most common response was, "Do I look as if I give a darn?" I wondered why pastors stroked one another's egos to make each other feel good and bragged to one another about who could out-do the other when they came together. I have many times witnessed firsthand situations where certain pastors evaluated the success of their sermon by the size of the offering that was collected.

I say this with all respect, but I have to be honest. I cannot tolerate this culture. It is a self-centered and self-serving one and is not at all about the people. When I tell you that God has called me to do this work, I mean it. He has not only called me, but He has allowed me opportunities to observe pastors as well as businessmen behind closed doors.

I have seen other pastors who spend most of their time with marketplace leaders, and I rather enjoy their company. I find it much easier to be around pastors who understand that the sheep are to be equipped and sent out into the marketplace. They understand that the marketplace leaders, or Kings, play a very important role in the Kingdom of God. These pastors do not try to hustle the businessmen nor do they try to impress others. They do not need to, for they know their role and how to walk alongside a King for the building of the Kingdom of God. These are the real pastors.

This book is not intended to undermine or devalue the important role that real pastors have played in the lives of so many as shepherds to God's sheep. Many of us have been helped directly or indirectly by someone who operates under the gift of a pastor, prophet, evangelist, teacher or apostle. We should thank God for giving the Body of Christ these gifts.

There are very distinct differences between a priest and a King. To my knowledge, these differences have seldom fully been addressed in the Black church. It is my intention in this book to uncover the understanding of each of these roles, how they affect their communities, and how to bring our communities back in the proper alignment with what the Lord intended. Over the many years before Christ and since the crucifixion and resurrection, man has tried to exalt himself over his brothers. When one person attempts to exalt himself over other people in the place reserved only for Jesus, the ordained order is destroyed.

My desire in writing this book is to remove any spiritual misunderstandings and expose any person and anything that prevents the Body of Christ from knowing the Master through His intended and appointed model of leadership.

God has ordained His people to have a King. This goes back to the book of Genesis 14 to Saul, who was given authority to govern the Israelites and rule on behalf of the Kingdom. Do not make the mistake of thinking God wants someone other than Himself to rule over His people. I am simply referring to ruling over the territory. The only one to decree something in the land, and the one with the biggest influence on the people was the King. In contemporary terms, a King is a businessperson, a political figure, an influencer or a marketplace leader. The impact of a God-directed King is in the marketplace. The impact of a pastor or priest is in equipping the sheep. Together, both fulfilling the calling of their ministry, they impact the community in powerful ways. They have a God-ordained interdependence; however, we must understand the difference between these mantles of authority and learn to operate in them according to God's will.

Satan can, in some cases, use Kings to further his agenda. Just look at the condition of the land and who is able to influence this satanic behavior. I challenge you to look at companies like Disney, Apple, Google, Facebook, Yahoo, and Target, as well as political figures and industry leaders in finance, media, education, government, sports and other fields to see where their beliefs lie. Satan's demons are not simply about possessing a person, they are directed to affect territory. If you understand the angelic realm, you know the assignments given to angels for individuals, cities, states, nations, continents and earth. Demons are fallen angels and their tasks are to affect the territory for Satan.

This book is designed to bring revelation of the true role of a pastor or priest and a King or businessman, in order to bring true alignment back to the Body. I use the term "priest" throughout this book to represent anyone called to the five-fold ministry (pastor, evangelist, teacher, prophet or apostle).

While I use the male form of these words, I mean to include women who are truly called into these positions. The Old English word *cwen* means "companion." It shows that the Queen's role was very different from the King's—that of friend, supporter, adviser or deputy. So, "Queen" is not really an appropriate title for a woman who does a King's job. That is why Queen Elizabeth I of England announced to her troops in 1588:

> *"I know I have the body of a weak and feeble woman, but I have the heart and stomach of a King, and of a King of England too. I think foul scorn that Parma or Spain, or any prince of Europe, should dare to invade the borders of my realm; to which, rather than*

*any dishonor should grow by me, I myself will
take up arms—I myself will be your general,
judge and rewarder of every one of your virtues
in the field."*

Elizabeth knew very well that she was the King of England. More than four centuries later, historians still recognize her as one of the best Kings who ever sat on England's throne. She had her share of "Queens" who offered advice, support and friendship—and most of them were male! In the same Elizabethan spirit, in this book, we will use the word "King" to refer to Kings of both genders.

This book is designed to deal with the issue of the destruction of our marketplace leaders by the traditional religious model of the Church. The believers' assault on the kingly anointing has been intentional by many who do not desire believers to understand their rightful authority in Christ. The same can be said about those clergy who have established themselves as the only voice of God while leaving the sheep without food and undermining the need for sheep to walk as marketplace leaders.

The people of God must come to know a Kingdom reality to prepare fully for and fulfill our purpose upon the earth. This dynamic must be set straight, especially for African-American people, who have absolutely no chance of ever emerging from the shambles in which we find ourselves, until we remove many of our pastors from positions of leadership in our communities.

It is my hope that the Kings will arise and understand their God-given role and authority to impact the marketplace. The priest or pastor has an important role to play in shepherding the sheep and also in counseling and advising the marketplace Kings. When this relationship is working properly, a kingdom will exist that reflects the Kingdom of God, and the powers of the enemy will not prevail. Many of our communities are lacking Kings and relying on priests to lead, with results that are totally destroying the people. I will also identify where many future Kings are located and how to release them into their rightful place.

We are running out of time and losing too many people due to our pride and desire to control others. Our eyes and hearts must be opened to receive what God is saying to His people. We must be willing to leave our traditions and former methods and allow God's will to be at the forefront. It is time for the priests and the Kings to come together to carry out the will of God as it was designed.

The tradition of how we have been taught to practice Christianity is what I am coming after. The results of lack of unity, high poverty, broken families, government dependence, entertainment focus, and spiritual immaturity reflect that the Kingdom has not come to the Black church.

> *Beware lest any man spoil you through philosophy and vain deceit, after the tradition of men, after the rudiments of the world, and not after Christ.* (Colossians 2:8, KJV)

He that has an ear to hear, let him hear what the Spirit is saying to the churches!

CHAPTER ONE

The Original Franchise

As a businessperson looking from an entrepreneurial perspective, I see that Jesus created what I would call the Original Franchise. Jesus set the foundation for the Father-intended way of doing things for all other "franchisees" or followers to model. Jesus, the High Priest, founded His work on a marketplace model of ministry that exists outside of the physical walls of a building.

Jesus first chose disciples who were successful businessmen from the marketplace: fishermen, carpenters, farmers and tax collectors. Jesus walked with marketplace leaders. As Christians, we deem ourselves to be "Christ-like," and to model the behavior of Christ. If a person is called to be a pastor or to operate in any five-fold ministry, then he should do what Jesus—the Original Franchisor—did and walk along side sheep and leaders. Jesus spent most of His time in the marketplace. If the Original Franchisor spent most of His time in the marketplace, then why don't present-day pastors? In addition, in most of His teachings, Jesus used marketplace parables or stories that illustrated agricultural exchange, which was the primary form of business in the days that Jesus walked the earth.

Yet we do not use a marketplace model today. The results that Jesus achieved have been unparalleled throughout the history of the world. If one wants to know why he is not getting the results of the Original Franchise, it is time to return to the operating manual.

As a former Ford and Buick car dealership owner, I have an intricate understanding of the franchise model. The sole purpose of planting a franchise is to represent a particular brand to the market. The franchisee is given the authority to use the respected name or brand. It makes no sense to use the name and then not follow the franchise's operating procedures.

When Ford appointed Mr. Pyrite as a franchisee, he began with good intentions. But he was ambitious, and he couldn't help noticing that his colleague Mr. Truman held the next franchise in a larger building. So Mr. Pyrite copied Mr. Truman's marketing campaigns, and the strategy seemed to be working. Soon his customer base increased. He earned more money and was able to employ more staff. He could buy a larger home and even a yacht, and his face appeared on all the commercials. He was becoming a big businessman!

Since material possessions and worldly acclaim were Mr. Pyrite's motivation, he lost sight of the Ford procedures. One day, he allowed some faulty warranty claims to be processed. Then he began to add larger profits per transaction. At the same time, he punished the customers by putting more and more of them into longer inequity positions. His whole career was now perverted by his self-serving greed. This craving to bolster his own ego, when he should have been leading and blessing his employees and customers, was what caused Mr. Pyrite's downfall.

He created his own warranty company for pre-owned vehicles but told the clients it was backed by the Ford brand. When Ford discovered this act of corruption, Mr. Pyrite was removed as a franchisee, and he lost everything. Unfortunately, this is a true story.

When the franchisee deviates from the operating procedures, the franchise is not being honestly represented. If you want to do it your own way, why bother with the franchise name? Simply do it your way and declare yourself independent of any franchise.

Jesus ushered in what I call the Kingdom Franchise. The Church of today should be following this Kingdom Franchise—but it is severely falling short.

The Kingdom Franchise

The Original Franchisor, Jesus, created the Kingdom Franchise. It reflects what Christ did when He walked the Earth. The reason why Jesus came down from Heaven and modeled this walk for three and a half years was to demonstrate how we are supposed to operate in and through the Kingdom.

There are many aspects of the Kingdom Franchise that Jesus created worth mentioning. The first is that a Kingdom Franchise has a priority of **pursuing the lost**. That is what Jesus did. His example to us was: "For the Son of Man came to seek and to save the lost" (Luke 19:10, AMP); and His commission to us is "Go and make disciples of all nations" (Matthew 28:19, KJV). Or, to summarize both the example and the commission:

> *When He saw the crowds, He had compassion on them, because they were harassed and help-less, like sheep without a shepherd. Then He said to his disciples, "The harvest is plentiful but the workers are few. Ask the Lord of the harvest, therefore, to send out workers into His harvest field."* (Matthew 9:36-38, NIV)

By going to the lost first, the franchise always has disciples being prepared and readied to be released.

The next stage of what Jesus did was to **introduce a new Kingdom**. When He went into a place, that place recognized that it was being introduced to something new:

> *News about Him spread all over Syria, and people brought to Him all who were ill with various diseases, those suffering severe pain, the demon-possessed, those having seizures, and the paralyzed; and He healed them. Large crowds from Galilee, the Decapolis, Jerusalem,*

Judea and the region across the Jordan followed him. (Matthew 4:24-25, NIV)

The people always recognized the new Kingdom that Jesus brought because the darkness became filled with light. Healing, the casting out of devils, the raising of the dead, and revelation and transformation happens when a Kingdom Franchise arrives.

God designed the believer, not the worship center, to be a Kingdom Franchise. What is the franchise blueprint for developing the believers into Kingdom Franchises?

> ... to **equip** His people for **works of service**, so that the body of Christ may be **built up** until we all **reach unity** in the faith and in the knowledge of the Son of God and **become mature**, attaining to the whole measure of the fullness of Christ. (Ephesians 4:12-13, NIV)

When the focus is on the activity of the worship center and not on yielding the same result that Jesus modeled, (which we have the power and authority to do by way of the Holy Spirit), then the center is operating in a way that does not reflect the King or the Franchisor. The operator is not following the operating manual, which is the Word. Whenever we move away from the operating manual, our results change, becoming more and more different from the results of the Original Franchise. What is the dangerous outcome for those worship centers that abandon the Kingdom Franchise? The "sheep" are likely to remain

*... infants, tossed back and forth by the waves,
and blown here and there by every wind
of teaching and by the cunning and crafti-
ness of people in their deceitful scheming....*
(Ephesians 4:14, NIV)

Prior to the Lord's sending the of Kingdom Franchise, there was darkness and fatherlessness. When you
truly have a Kingdom Franchise, the Lord brings you
out of darkness and fatherlessness to be transformed to
His likeness. He then instructs you to go out and represent this new franchise right in your primary market
area (PMA). He sends you to be His witness and
declare His Word. Since you are from that "market,"
you know how others in that PMA think and act.

How will you know a true Kingdom Franchise?
You will recognize it by the operator's knowledge of
what the people need, since he used to be in the same
situation as those people who most need the Lord.

The Kingdom Franchise should be planted in
places where people need the food of the Word of God
and are hurting and lost. Just as a present-day business
franchisor designates primary market areas (PMAs) for
their operations, the Kingdom Franchises should also
be set on a PMA. This creates a system by which a franchisor identifies franchisees to be placed all around the
market to represent and bring their products, services
and brand to the people. You can always tell when a
franchise is owned by someone who doesn't know the
market—the decor and way of operating says they do
not know their customer.

When you buy a franchise, one of the things that your corporation requires is that you live in the territory to which you are assigned. Why is that? They need you to know that area. A franchise expands and grows when it is in an area with which the owner or operator is familiar and involved.

A franchisor can say that he wants a particular area that looks potentially profitable, but that does not mean that it is to be his PMA. Some PMAs are larger than others. You give a certain franchisee a larger market after he has shown himself faithful in a smaller market. You never give a big market to a new franchise. You promote someone who has already shown that he can operate in your system and obtain the organization's desired result, and then you offer him a new opportunity.

This is how Ford did it when I was in the car dealership business. Ford would say they had a bigger opportunity they would like to offer a promising franchisee, but they required that he must first sell his current franchise. The reason they would do this is that the larger opportunity required them to take a risk on the franchisee, even though he had already succeeded in a smaller market. They did not want to have their new operator distracted. If the new franchisee was all about pride, money and greed, then he would say he wanted to keep his old franchise and also have the new one. This request was only possible if there was a disciple who could continue to operate under the same discipline, hence freeing the leader to move on to a larger market. The market penetration was not expected to decrease while the new larger market was awarded. Someone had to make sure the customers of the old franchise continued to receive the intended experience of the franchisor.

Pastors who operate in greed, pride and selfishness behave in this same manner. They say that they want more church buildings: "one church, ten locations." They hold back the very gifts in which other people have been called to operate because they want personal control. These pastors want so much control that they will board a helicopter after they preach at one service to reach the next service at the other location, leaving both locations with no real shepherding. Their agenda is to control the whole market area—a monopoly. They want to control and manipulate the franchise model, and the sheep just have to deal with it. They believe their teaching and worship center model is the product. I contend the product is the Kingdom and the vessels or buildings are His people. This explains why so much focus is on new locations and ministry expansion, since the product being promoted is their ministry.

A true Kingdom Franchisor willingly gives up his role at the old territory, allowing someone else's promotion, so that he can devote himself to the needs of his new congregation. A true shepherd will want the Master's sheep to know what it is like to keep growing and expanding. He wants to be like Jesus, and he knows that this is what Jesus did.

The Kingdom Franchise—the Body of Christ— must understand that it is representing a corporate establishment that has a tested and proven model, the example of Christ and the Word of God. If the model was not tested and proven, then why did you buy into it in the first place?

Think about it. I was not awarded a Ford franchise by saying that I planned to go ahead and do it my way. I had to go through some Ford processes so the franchisers could see that I had been taught the Ford model and could operate within it. People want to buy the franchise with the tested and proven model. People will not buy a supposed franchise with a brand that is producing bad product. The brand of the franchise is always displayed out front to let you know that this store represents the trusted brand owner. All McDonald's restaurants have logos, and if the logo is not there, it lets you know that this restaurant is not a McDonald's.

Remember that old Eddie Murphy movie *Coming to America*? There was an artificial franchise, McDowell's, trying to copy the ways of McDonald's. The owner took what he could glean from McDonald's operating manual and did his own thing. When questioned about the differences between McDowell's and McDonald's, he had answers, but not strong ones. He made minor changes to McDonald's products, and passed them off as his own (the Big Mac vs. the Big Mick). He was trying to be McDonald's without following the process.

A franchise is a duplicable model. If you follow the instructions of the franchise manual, you produce the intended results. In one of my corporate roles, I ensured that the franchisees stayed in line with the policies and procedures of the franchisor.

Mr. Bigg was a corporate employee who understood the franchise model. He understood it so well that he was able to use his corporate position to trick a Ford franchisee out of his franchise. Then he took possession of this prime location for himself.

Mr. Bigg, now turned dealer, chose to disregard the operating manual. He built up a kingdom by manipulating his customers and controlling his employees. He used many gimmicks and gambits designed to create huge sales and profits. He flaunted his connections in the Old School network as he demanded special treatment from corporate representatives: cut prices, free tickets, the best table in the restaurants, whatever. If the reps failed to deliver, Mr. Bigg would remind them of his influence over the top executives and of his control over their growth. He had the power to alienate anyone who did not serve his agenda.

Although his threats and arrogance earned him a bad reputation in his assigned market area, that did not bother him, for he sold most of his vehicles to people from surrounding areas. He pumped customers from other dealer-markets into his own by retailing products that were under-supplied in other dealers' inventories. His sales did not reflect his performance as a better operator but his manipulation of corporate people. Another word for "manipulation" is just plain "bullying."

Mr. Bigg might have bullied his customers, colleagues and employees right up to the day of his multi-million dollar retirement if Ford had not undergone a regime change. The new CEO removed the old brass from the top executive positions and replaced them with his own disciples. As most of them were from Europe, they were completely disconnected from America's Old School culture. These new executives were totally unimpressed by people like Mr. Bigg. When they called the franchisees to account, their only concern was *market share*: How well are you representing Ford?

The new executives quickly figured out that Mr. Bigg was not selling to people in his own market area and that his substandard reputation was giving Ford a negative image. They deliberately set up a plan to remove him. My boss went to Mr. Bigg's dealership and served notice that he must measure up to the Ford standard or else he would be evicted. Long story short, Mr. Bigg was unable to recoup his misdeeds, and he was forced to sell out.

The replacement dealer represents the Ford brand accurately by operating under Fords' policies and procedures. His franchise is extremely profitable, and it is steadily increasing Ford's market share.

What does a corporation do when a franchise is not operating properly? What does it have the right to do? It has the right to terminate the sales and service agreement. The company can come and take down its brand or remove the franchisee's ability to use its name. Of course, a few people will still come into a disenfranchised store without recognizing that the franchise has been removed and is no longer operating, but those people are being cheated.

In the same way, if you accept the Jesus of the Bible, surely you trust what He said and intend to do what He tells you to do. Following an alternative plan doesn't make any sense. In this case, the model that is being represented in the franchise is that of the Kingdom of Heaven. This, and nothing else, is what needs to be represented in the primary assigned territory. We must follow the model that Jesus showed us. Jesus has given us the authority to use His name. Being His disciple means following Him closely. We can only obtain the desired results by duplicating His model.

> *Whatever you ask in my name, this I will do, that the Father may be glorified in the Son. If you ask me anything in my name, I will do it.* (John 14:13-14, NIV)

The role of the shepherd (and the other elders) is to make sure that the Body of Christ stays in line with Jesus' operating plan in every area of life. This means sleeping and eating habits, thoughts and words, family life and friendships, money and time—everything.

> *Speaking the truth in love, we will grow to become in every respect the mature body of Him who is the head, that is, Christ. From Him the whole body, joined and held together by every supporting ligament, grows and builds itself up in love, as each part does its work.* (Ephesians 4:15-16, NIV)

A caretaker knows not to sleep in his master's bed. He does not own the house; he is there to take care of it. He serves the master in order to further the master's agenda. But a squatter will invade a house and help himself to anything he likes. He eats the master's food, wears his clothes, watches his television and sleeps in his bed. The squatter's only hope is that the master will never come home!

In the same way, a usurping priest "squats" in God's house to further his own agenda. His intention is to steal the house for himself, so you will find him sleeping in the master bedroom. He puts his wife and children on payroll. The elders are his friends or people under his control. He tells the sheep that it is their duty to pay for his house and be his servants. Whenever his doors open, the sheep are supposed to be there. He invites his buddies to come and make money off the sheep (a circuit or group tour). The buddies can be trusted never to rock the boat, since he will soon be doing a similar favor for them. So he demands endless servitude from the very people whom he is supposed to be serving.

Has he forgotten that the Master *will* come home?

Yet this pastor-centered manipulation is happening throughout the Body of Christ today. It happens because people are "coming to Jesus" through emotion-alism or coercion and not the leading of the Spirit. In fact, of course, you shouldn't come to Jesus by joining a congregation and becoming excited about a pastor. You come to Jesus by repenting of your sins and trusting in His forgiveness. When naïve people join a congregation without understanding this, they need help in bringing their lives in line with the operating manual.

People continue to enter the building, not realizing that the Original Franchise is no longer operating. Hungry people are being served the pastor's food, not the Master's. They are still asking to be fed, but the brand has changed. We should all watch out and observe which franchise we are entering! Too many churches today are offering a counterfeit brand with counterfeit agendas, no longer even operating by the guidelines of the original manual—the Holy Bible.

It is killing the sheep and destroying the Kings.

CHAPTER TWO

The King

Throughout history, Kings have had very distinct roles. Kings provided oversight of running and maintaining the province, territory or country over which he had been given authority and ownership. The King oversaw the setting of tax rates, establishing religious order, electricity, census of the territory, maintaining agricultural status, overseeing business in the land and building relationships with other elected officials. The King made sure those in his court were suitable for their roles. Most Kings were called to have their castles built inside gated walls to protect the castle's inhabitants from raids during wars. Kings were also expected to have a Queen or next of kin to keep their kingdom intact while the King was away at war or ill.

It is now the role of a modern-day King to lead and build a "kingdom." The King understands the role he plays, which is to build a thriving community that includes businesses, education centers, living establishments, worship centers, organizations that serve the community and an infrastructure for growth. He is to take care of the needs of the poor, orphans, widows and seniors in the kingdom. All this is done while seeking to conquer more territory. A true King—or business leader—understands that his role is critical to the well-being of his community. A King knows that he influences politicians, teachers, the people and all who are in that kingdom.

Years ago, I watched the movie *Rome* on H.B.O. In this movie, Caesar understood that he would be evaluated by the people on how much they grew and prospered under his leadership. As a businessman, I have learned to evaluate my success in relation to the growth of the people working under me and not just by the bottom line of my business. The mind of the King should be on the growth and protection of the people within his territory.

Kings Create Communities

If you are a King, you must recognize that your role is to build a kingdom where the people have a greater chance to prosper not just financially, but also within their families and community. The role of the King is to receive "downloads" or insights from God in the form of ideas, vision, or the ability to anticipate potential for future opportunities. Included in that vision are the gifts and callings of others.

One such King was Charles Fraser. He saw twelve miles of unspoiled beach on Hilton Head Island, SC, and bought enough land to develop the gated holiday-makers' community of Sea Pines Resort. Its success encouraged other developers to build similar resorts that imitated Fraser's plan and style. The tourist industry spurred the growth of cultural activities: multiple golf courses, an Arts Center for live theater, a choral society, a symphony orchestra and several community festivals. Charles Fraser was a committed environmentalist who changed the whole configuration of the marina to save an ancient oak. To this day, with its original population now increased a hundredfold, Hilton Head Island retains a very high level of tree cover relative to buildings. Hilton Head, SC, is considered by many to be a world-class community where a high quality of life is expected.

The moviemaker Walt Disney was also a King whose vision included the callings of many others. [1]He was the first to exploit new techniques in the movie industry: sound, color, the multi-plane camera. He presented the world with Mickey Mouse in *Steamboat Willie* in 1928 and with *Snow White* in 1937. Disney had his own studio in 1940, but most of the facilities were devoted to the war effort. His films for the armed services included training, propaganda, health advice and short comedies to boost morale. After the war, he made many educational documentaries about wild-life and conservation. It was at his instigation that two

---

1 www.justdisney.com

local colleges were amalgamated to create the California Institute of Arts, a place where all the creative and performing arts could be taught under one roof in a "community of the arts," which at the time was a completely new approach to professional arts training. In 1955 he invested $17 million into the first Disneyland theme park, the Magic Kingdom, which soon returned its investment tenfold. Ten years later, with a new vision to improve urban life in America, he designed an Experimental Prototype Community of Tomorrow (EPCOT) and directed the purchase of 43 square miles of unused land in the center of Florida. He master-planned a new world of entertainment to include a new Disney theme park, a motel-hotel vacation resort center and his EPCOT. Although Disney died the following year, Walt Disney World opened in 1971 and the EPCOT Center in 1982. The tourist traffic to Florida has never ceased since, and today tourism to the Walt Disney World Resort, comprised of more than 25,000 acres—nearly 30 resorts and six theme and water parks—it is the staple industry of the state.

In this same way, the King will provide a way for others who desire to own businesses. Whether it is dry cleaners, resorts, restaurants, law offices or any other type of business that can directly benefit from the vision of a King, the goal is to establish these businesses to prosper.

A King understands that in order to rule properly, he must create an environment of serving others. A true business leader understands his role is not just to make money and to write checks but also to be involved on boards of social organizations and to be the catalyst by which the community grows. This responsibility of a King is given to him by God, not by man. Kings understand the importance of serving in a community. A King also understands the importance of the people within their companies serving others. This is why most companies give incentives to encourage employees to volunteer in the community.

The Authority of a King

Let everyone be subject to the governing authorities, for there is no authority except that which God has established. The authorities that exist have been established by God. Consequently, whoever rebels against the authority is rebelling against what God has instituted, and those who do so will bring judgment on themselves. For rulers hold no terror for those who do right, but for those who do wrong. Do you want to be free from fear of the one in authority? Then do what is right and you will be commended. For the one in authority is God's servant for your good. But if you do wrong, be afraid, for rulers do not bear the sword for no reason. They are God's servants, agents of wrath to bring punishment on the wrongdoer. Therefore, it is necessary to submit to the authorities, not only because of possible punishment but also as a matter of conscience. (Romans 13:1-5, NIV)

He changes times and seasons; he sets up kings and deposes them. He gives wisdom to the wise and knowledge to the discerning. (Daniel 2:21, NIV)

A King is ordained by God to walk in authority, to receive vision and to lead the kingdom in the ways of God. The power given to a King is one of dominion and ultimate responsibility. A King's authority is something in which he abides by and operates in throughout his kingdom. His authority is not something that needs to be emphasized to others by constantly stressing his title, posting his face on billboards, writing his name on buildings, or throwing pictures of himself on the walls.

A King's authority is reflected in whatever he rules or governs and keeps under his jurisdiction. Because of the responsibility given to a King, the condition of the kingdom sits on his shoulders. Jesus was the model for this understanding. In Isaiah 9:6 (NIV) it says:

> For a child is born to us, a son is given to us. The **government** will rest on His **shoulders**. And He will be called: Wonderful Counselor, Mighty God, Everlasting Father, Prince of Peace.

A King's authority is not subject to anyone in his kingdom other than those who gave him the power to rule or to another kingdom that has more power and authority. A King is never higher than his God. I love it when the Bible tells us that Jesus will return as King of Kings and Lord of Lords (I Timothy 6:15, Revelation 17:14). This tells me that His Kingdom is the ultimate authority, and if I submit my kingdom to His Kingdom, I access the authority of His Kingdom when my authority is depleted.

A King who puts his kingdom under the Kingdom of God will rule with all power and authority. Until a King comes into the measure of the stature of the fullness of Christ (Ephesians 4:13) there is a limit to a King's marketplace effectiveness. A King will only be effective to the extent that he is subject to the Kingdom of God.

A King must always exercise his authority. A King has the power to release his authority to those whom he chooses to operate on his behalf. I will call these people "managers," since they have been given authority to lead a department, organization or people. Even with some of the work delegated to his managers, ultimate responsibility still sits on the shoulders of the King.

The Bible tells of a Centurion who came to Jesus and said that he had a sick servant at home. Jesus told him that He would come to his house with him. The Centurion said, "No, you don't have to come to my house; all You have to do is speak a word." He said he was also a man of authority and when he told a soldier to go, the soldier went and did whatever he ordered. This worldly King instinctively recognized the King of Kings, a man of even greater authority than himself. The Bible says that Jesus marveled at him and said there was no greater faith in all of Israel than what this man had shown (Matthew 8: 5-13, KJV; Luke 7:2-10, KJV). Jesus knew that the one who could understand him best is the one who understands authority and who walks in authority.

Satan also knows this, and that is why he attacks people who have been anointed in a kingly capacity. He knows that if he can destroy the King, he can destroy and control the people. You must understand this part of a King's power. While Jesus gave authority to the disciples, He knew that He carried the full responsibility for the Body of Christ. Jesus says:

> *I give you the **authority** to trample on serpents and scorpions, and over all the power of the enemy, and nothing shall by any means hurt you.* (Luke 10:19, KJV).

Jesus, who was King and Priest, gives authority to His disciples (managers), but the responsibility for the sheep remained on His shoulders.

Jesus made a statement to His disciples when they argued over who was the greatest by saying in Luke 22:25 (NIV), *"The kings of the Gentiles exercise lordship over them, and those who exercise authority over them are the 'benefactors'."* This scripture illustrates that in the marketplace, the Kings have lordship but delegate authority to others. Whether you are a Jew or Gentile is not the issue here. It is the point of understanding the authority of a King that is important.

A King understands that his authority reaches out to the borders of his kingdom and no farther. When a King moves outside of his area of dominion, his authority leaves, and he is now subject to another King. A King knows there is only one way to change the borders of his kingdom. He must take over another area or neighboring land in battle (gentrification is a physical example). A battle is then waged between Kings, for no one but a King can declare war. A King must consider expanding his dominion from his home to his business, his community, city, state, region, country, and then the world.

A Glimpse into the Mindset of a King

We must identify the Kings. Once you understand how the mind of a King works, you will recognize if that ten-year-old in your house, that eighteen-year-old on the corner, or that fifty-year-old man sitting in a prison cell is really a King. You must grasp how a King thinks. Since most people do not know any true Kings, they end up mistaking a priest for a King. As a result, you want the King to sound like a priest. And this, my friend, will not happen. Reconsider your concept of a King, and then you can be exposed to real Kings.

The first thing you must understand about the mind of a King is that he operates in a mindset of **authority**. He does not sound like wavering or indecisive people. He does not sit on the fence about issues. He does not sound very soft in his presentation and he does not and will not entertain you. The only ones who set out to entertain are clowns. Clowns entertain; Kings walk in authority.

You can tell a King by his usually serious nature. This does not mean that he is not jovial at times or is not a gregarious person. But, an overall characteristic is that he has a serious nature about him. He understands that there is more going on than the obvious here-and-now, and most of his thoughts are geared toward moving forward. As a result, he will usually seem focused.

The second thing to understand about the mindset of a King is that he doesn't want to merely have a presence. He wants to **take over**. He doesn't have a *"let me just build my little building right here, so I can get mine"* mentality. A King has a *"what do I need to do to rule"* mentality. A King thinks with a **take-over** mentality.

I saw an example of this in the movie *New Jack City*. Nino Brown, played by Wesley Snipes, was the leader of an up-and-coming gang who devised a new product. (Unfortunately, it was crack cocaine.) He then said to the group around him, at the board table, that they were going to come off like the mob and take over the Carter, a local public housing complex. One of his men said to Nino, "You're not thinking of taking over the Carter, are you?" Nino replied with authority and without hesitation, "Yes, we're taking over the Carter". This was a demonstration of the mindset of a King. A King is not meant to only have a presence in a particular area. He is designed to take over.

This is why you hear our misguided young men leading their gangs and saying that they don't just want to have a presence in a neighborhood. They intend to take over entire blocks. This is why a businessman doesn't just say that he wants to be a part of an industry. He wants to dominate that industry.

A King understands that he wants to take over, so he designates a territory. That territory may be from block A–C. If another King states that he already owns blocks D–F, the first King, determined to grow his kingdom, declares battle with the rival King's territory. A King's mindset is not to just have presence or to blend in; it is to take over or dominate.

The third thing to grasp about the way the mind of a King works is that he knows he must corral or **gather people**. He must bring people together around him. Think about the drug dealers and the gang bangers who are out there. One of the things at which they are very good is recruiting. They understand how to tap into the minds and needs of people. They know that there are communities full of boys with no fathers, so they present themselves as a family and father-figure. It's not hard to figure out. Any businessman knows that he will succeed to the degree that he is able to keep around him good people who produce results.

When a King corrals people to be around him, he brings soldiers and others who know how to get a job done without any excuses or shortfalls. He gathers people who have different gifts and talents that will further his kingdom. The King does not try to control it all. He delegates and empowers those he has gathered around him. He knows that control is for weak-minded people. You can identify a weak-minded person by the way he usually only gathers his family, friends or deficient people around him. That is a weak excuse for a leader. A real King's mind brings around him people who have the capacity and standard to accomplish the assignment of creating a thriving kingdom or community.

A King **demands total obedience** from those gathered around him. Why? He knows there is order in obedience. This is something that most people will never understand, for most people run away from and buck against any authority. However, people who do this will never grow. God has given different levels of authority to different people. Mature people can distinguish between different levels of authority. When I recognize someone of great authority, I have no problem submitting to him. But I will never submit to false kings or pastors who hustle the people and walk around as the leaders of the community. No! I see easily that they are operating outside of God's order, and we must break away from that.

While writing this book, I read *Outwitting the Devil* by Napoleon Hill, written in 1938 but not published until 2011. Although Hill is most famous for his best-selling book *Think and Grow Rich*, [2] I found some better descriptions in *Outwitting* of a King (a "non-drifter"). He mentions these personality traits on pages 93-94.

- The tone of his voice, the quickness of his step, the sparkle in his eyes, the quickness of his decisions clearly mark him as a person who knows exactly what he wants and is deter-

---

2 Hill, Napoleon, 1883-1970 and Sharon L. Lechter. 2011. *Outwitting the Devil: The Secret to Freedom and Success.* New York: Sterling Ethos.

mined to get it, no matter how long it may take or what price he must pay.

- If you ask him questions, he gives you direct answers and never falls back on evasions or resorts to subterfuge.

- He extends many favors to others, but accepts favors sparingly or not at all.

- He will be found up front, whether he is playing a game or fighting a war.

- If he does not know the answers, he will say so frankly.

- He has a good memory.

- He never offers an alibi for his shortcomings.

- He never blames others for his mistakes, no matter if they deserve the blame.

- He used to be known as a "go-getter," but in modern times, he is called a "go-giver." You will find him running the biggest business in town, living on the best street, driving the best automobile and making his presence felt wherever he happens to be.

- He is an inspiration to all who come into contact with his mind.

- The major distinguishing feature of a non-drifter [King] is this: he has a mind of his own and uses it for all purposes.

The Language of a King

A King has a distinguished language. He is most often very direct and to the point. He is not interested in fluff or emotional behavior. A King understands his position of authority and the value of time, so he is very efficient in his communication. He also will not be called to participate in the game of ego or manipulation that small talk or idle chat can instigate. The language of a King can also be course, very direct, upfront or "in your face," and he doesn't waste a lot of words.

I have found Kings to be unapologetic for their aggressiveness or personality. They don't have to apologize for who they are. They understand the need for their kingly mindset. A King needs to be clear in the direction and instruction given to those around his table. A King does not lead by democracy, even though he understands the importance of including the counsel of those who are around his table. Even with input, he sees the vision God has given him, and usually will not compromise on carrying out that vision.

A King is very direct and focused on the vision or goal at hand. Napoleon Hill's book *Outwitting the Devil* refers to people with this "definiteness of purpose" as "non-drifters." We often call them type A personalities, but I would like to refer to them as "dominion operators." The many leadership books on very successful marketplace leaders will almost always sound totally different from the books written by non-Kings. The voice of a King speaks with authority, for he understands the power behind his words. The understanding of authority is critical to a King, as well as how to handle someone who does not respect his authority. You and I must understand that a King sounds different, speaks in authority and has a take-over mindset.

You will notice that a King has little tolerance for people who lack respect for authority because he knows a kingdom without respect for authority will always fall. Take a look at Matthew 7:28–29 (NIV), a verse that speaks to this:

> *And so it was, when Jesus had ended these sayings, that people were astonished at His teaching, for He taught them as one having authority, and not as the scribes.*

I love this scripture. A marketplace King loves the authority of Christ. It is not the weak teaching we sometimes see in today's church. It is not some false rhythmic pronunciation of his words or stretching out words. You've heard it: "Gawd" meaning God or "Jesusssss" meaning Jesus or "Mand of God" meaning Man of God.

A King understands the importance of sounding confident and not wavering when speaking to others. A King knows the power of his words and can easily be construed as spineless if he sounds double-minded or lacking in certainty. A King will always listen to others who know their language, especially those who do not use phrases like,

"I might…"

"I was thinking about…"

"I was going to…"

"Maybe…"

or words that seem to be indecisive. A King loves the words of Jesus, who did not sound apologetic, not even when His truth offended the religious leaders of his time. A King's language will be considered abrasive to many non-leaders due to the enabling spirit that most people carry.

I remember introducing a colleague to my business mentor some years ago. It took less than one minute for my mentor to offend my colleague totally. When I later asked my colleague what the problem was, he stated, "He asked me all these questions and then looked at me as if I was crazy when I did not respond. He was so rude! He just walked away while I was thinking of my response."

I laughed to myself. I then realized that in the realm of kingdom business, I had just introduced a commoner to a King. I had forgotten that commoners are always offended by total authority. It was not that my mentor did anything wrong. It was that I put someone around him who should never have been in his presence. It was my fault for not understanding that what I loved the most about my mentor was what others would dislike about him: his unapologetic and direct authority. A King is not cut from the same cloth as a non-king.

A King's language always speaks to something bigger than himself. A King requires total obedience to his laws, processes and procedures, and so he usually speaks to the expectation more than to the person. A King speaks to what he *expects* of a position, person or thing and not to the thing. Think of when Jesus cursed the fig tree that did not produce what was expected (Matthew 21:18-22). A King understands speaking to expectations and not things.

A King does not enjoy being in the presence of someone who speaks the language of religious clichés. These clichés contain rhetorical devices and no authority. You've heard many of them:

"God is good and all the time, God is good."

"I know whose I am and who I am."

"I am blessed and highly favored of God."

"This is my season of blessings."

Not that any of these clichés are wrong, but they lack substance and show a lack of the true identity that comes from within. Prince Charles, heir to the British throne and son of Queen Elizabeth, would never walk into a room and use these kinds of clichés. He knows who he is, and that is enough for him and everyone else.

The language Jesus spoke upon the earth is totally attractive to the marketplace. There was no one who spoke in authority like Jesus. A true King will never sit under a shepherd teaching anything less than to operate in the authority in Christ that has been given to His people.

The Teachings of the King

A King teaches others with these steps:

- Information: expose me to something I did not know.

- Instruction: tell me how to apply this in my life.

- Application with accountability: show me how to apply and hold me accountable for the application in my life.

- Transformation: the exposure to your teaching has now become a part of my lifestyle/habit.

- Duplication: I teach others what you have taught me.

The only reason a King teaches anything is its application to bring about transformation. The measurement of true teaching is its test in life, which requires you to put into practice what you have been informed and instructed to do.

Examples of the teaching of kings are as follows:

Dave Ramsey, Financial Principles; John Maxwell, Leadership; Jim Rohn, Discipline; Warren Buffet, Investments; and Dr. James Dobson, Marriage and Family. You will see that the teachings of kings demand application of the student and not emotional appeal that causes no action.

I challenge you to think of a Black-Christian person who is not a pastor and who teaches on specific areas of living, outside of Oprah. In the Black church, the pastor tries to be the primary teacher from a pulpit while denying the gifts placed in the members of the body who would better equip the saints in that specific area of living.

The Discipline of the King

A King has a natural sense of discipline and order. He is disciplined in the way he runs his schedule, dresses and conducts himself. In most cases, you will notice a King is somewhat compulsive in his behavior, since he understands better than most the importance of structure.

If you think about the importance of discipline for a King, you will understand that this discipline must be reflected in all areas of his life. A King understands the importance of time and how precious time is to the productivity of his business and personal life. As I have said many times, show me a person who respects time, and I will show someone in position to lead. I will use an example to illustrate this point. A King knows that time is what employees have exchanged with him for a paycheck. The time needed to prosper is the same as the time needed to fail; however, the difference lies in what you do with the time you have available.

When I was running dealerships, I remember how important it was for a technician to be efficient in order to maximize billable time versus actual time needed to perform a job. Billable time says to a technician: "You may bill a customer 2.5 hours for this job, but if you finish in 2 hours, you could move on to another job." The technician is paid for 2.5 hours, although it only took two to complete. Imagine working eight hours, but you are paid for twelve. This is only done through focus, knowledge, structure and understanding of efficiency.

A King must also show discipline in his health, for everything else is affected by his eating and exercise habits. The insurance industry understands this very well when it is insuring a business or the "key man." You will very seldom see a King who is terribly out of shape and sickly. He knows he *must* be disciplined in this area. I know we all face challenges in this area, since we live in a sickly culture where both work and hobbies revolve around sedentary computer-based activities, and junk food is easily available. However, culture is no excuse for a King. Jesus was counter-cultural, and His disciples can be counter-cultural, too.

I challenge you to go to lunch at a restaurant that is mostly frequented by business leaders. See what they are eating and what is on the menu. I also recommend that you go to the local gyms early in the morning and ask the patrons what they do for a living. The other way to find out the health habits of Kings is to stop people who are jogging in the morning or late at night. You will find that they are more than likely business leaders.

A King's discipline is the very foundation of his success and must not be influenced by people who lack discipline in these and other key areas. When God gives vision to a King concerning anything, the discipline needed to build a kingdom is critical to the process. Kings truly understand the power of discipline in their personal lives and also in the kingdoms they govern.

When a King loses focus to distractions or by simply taking his eye off his businesses, the community will suffer. I have advised many Kings to be very careful when allowing non-Kings to be around them, since non-kings do not always operate in these very basic disciplines.

The Character of a King

A King's character should be founded on integrity, compassion, service and the understanding of the enormous responsibility given to him. A King must walk in integrity. If he does not operate with absolute integrity, the people he leads will be taken advantage of, and the community will suffer.

The character of a King also includes being compassionate. A King should lead with compassion for the lost and hurting and not be influenced or motivated to gain material wealth to simply take care of his own needs. A King must understand that the way he shows compassion is by creating a kingdom where those in need have opportunities to better their lives. While a King brings together those who can create better opportunities for those in need, he is careful not to bind them into a reality where they are taught to be dependent on others and feel entitled to receive without contributing.

The character of a King entails a natural understanding that he is there to serve those who place their confidence in him. He is constantly thinking of the people who are relying on his success for their livelihood. While the King's employees or kingdom citizens respect the King's authority, he knows that he is actually serving them.

When I purchased my first dealerships, I learned a very important lesson. I demanded that employees respect and respond to the authority of the organizational structure. With that in mind, I then insisted that those to whom authority had been delegated serve those over whom they had been placed. When an employee or kingdom citizen respects and serves the authority or title of a particular leadership position, the person who holds the leadership position actually works for the betterment of the employee.

I used to keep a particular employee in mind to always remind myself of this fact. I would always think of Harold, the janitor/detailer. I knew that if I kept Harold, who appeared to have a less important role, at the forefront of my mind, I would honor the value of all the employees whom I showed up every day to serve. I knew that every employee contributed to the overall success of each dealership. In return, they brought their best to their positions and produced stellar results.

Let us return to the story of the Centurion with the ailing servant. The Centurion, a true King, knew that in order for his servant to be at his best, he had to step in on that servant's behalf. He told Jesus that he was a man of authority to his people, and he was coming to get something for his servant that was outside of his servant's or his own authority. He came as an act of service to his own servant (see Matthew 8:5–13, NIV).

A marketplace King needs to understand this, so he never gets caught up on how much money he is making for himself and will always be sensitive to the needs of the community. The great Kings were evaluated on how much the people prospered while under their rule. A real King will deal with the condition of the people and the land. He does not want the people to be sick or suffer.

A King's character is also shaped by those who sit at his table. When you find a King or business leader who has been leading by greed and selfish desires, it is evident that this King has not been developed or counseled by godly people or priests.

This point is illustrated in Philippians 3:18–19 (KJV) when Paul says:

For many walk, of whom I have told you often, and now tell you even weeping, that they are the enemies of the cross of Christ: Whose end is destruction, whose god is their belly, and whose glory is in their shame, who mind earthly things.

When Paul is talking about the belly—our basal desires and instincts—as a god, he is highlighting our greed and the fact that we continue to feed our flesh. This is evidence of someone who is no longer putting God first, but has replaced the Lord's position with seeking after material goods. This path always ends in destruction.

Kings Have Great Discernment

Kings must have a strong sense of discernment to rule any kingdom effectively. God gives him this discernment, so he can sort through the requests that multiply daily and to make the right decisions for the kingdom.

Discernment—This gift equips one to know instinctively what is going on beyond the surface of a situation or an individual. Those with the gift of discernment have the ability to determine genuineness or phoniness. An example of leading through discernment is a person who judges that someone wants to be in a position of leadership out of a wrong motive (1 John 4:1-3).

I will add another definition to discernment: being able to identify the difference between good and God's will. You see, my struggle was not always the decision between good and evil but mostly between doing what I thought was good versus what the will of God, the Father, was for this situation.

For a true King, it is easy to sort through what is real and what is counterfeit. This is a gift in which a marketplace leader must operate. The same dynamic occurs with these young men in the streets and in prison. When you are with these young men, you see that they can sense any ulterior motives from those in front of them. These young men are always looking for the angle from which people are coming and very easily know how to respond. This sense of discernment is common amongst the best business leaders in the world. A King is focused on manifesting God's vision and has no time or tolerance for swindlers.

The Vision of a King

Vision is given to Kings. God revealed a dream to Pharaoh (King of Egypt) concerning the seven years of forthcoming famine in the land. The King was the one who had authority in the kingdom, so the dream was given to him (Genesis 41: 1-57).

Walt Disney, founder of the Walt Disney Company and King of the entertainment industry, believed very much in his vision to create a world of entertainment. [3]"The mission of The Walt Disney Company is to be one of the world's leading producers and providers of entertainment and information. Using

---

3 www.thewaltdisneycompany.com/investors

our portfolio of brands to differentiate our content, services and consumer products, we seek to develop the most creative, innovative and profitable entertainment experiences and related products in the world." Walt purchased 43 square miles of land in Florida and transformed swampland into one of the largest attractions in the world. Can you imagine a world without Disney? If you were able to ask Walt what he had in mind, I am sure he would say that we are seeing it manifest even after his death.

A King's vision encompasses many smaller assignments and vision that God gives to people within the kingdom. Consider how your vision as head of your organization affects all those under you. Can you see how the vision of the leader can positively or negatively affect the lives of the others in your organization? He will first give a King the vision that he is to establish a kingdom or community. Within that vision are the visions of doctors to have their own practices, teachers to be a part of the education system, elders to begin worship centers, facilities for exercise and recreation, clothing stores to outfit the people, dry cleaners to clean the clothes and all other forms of business that operate in any successful kingdom.

Consider the Kings or business leaders who had a vision for a town, city, organization or other entity and the impact the vision had on the area. Milton Hershey, founder of Hershey Chocolate Company, had a vision that we now see throughout Hershey, PA. This community in Pennsylvania consists of many smaller visionaries now given permission to come to Hershey to manifest their vision. Milton Hershey's vision continues to be the foundation of the area's prosperity.

Although both of these examples are large in scale, I am convinced all Kings have vision to influence their fields. The challenge is who will be their King, Jesus or Satan? What kind of influence will the people be under.

It has become more clear to me why Black Christians have so many worship centers, one on every block but no kingdom. The reason is pastors are competing for the territory by the presence of their worship centers. Sometimes, the larger the building, the more perceived the rule over the people is. How does this model improve the condition of the land for the people?

The Resources are for Kings

Before I continue, I'll let you know that this section may be shocking for most of you. This part of the book may offend many pastors and cause many believers to question the very foundation of this book.

Are these new ideas? No. Napoleon Hill understood them seventy years ago. [4]In *Outwitting the Devil*, Satan shares how he hates the Rockefeller fortune, and furthermore, how he loathes that any money should fall into the hands of Kings. On page 64, Satan claims:

---

4   Hill, Napoleon, 1883-1970 and Sharon L. Lechter. 2011. *Outwitting the Devil: The Secret to Freedom and Success.* New York: Sterling Ethos.

"The Rockefeller money is being used to isolate and conquer diseases of the physical body, in all parts of the world. The Rockefeller money is uncovering new secrets of nature in a hundred different directions, all of which are designed to help men take and keep possession of their own minds. It is encouraging new and better methods of feeding, clothing, and housing people. It is wiping out the slums in the large cities, the places where my favorite allies are found. It is financing campaigns for better government and helping to wipe out dishonesty in politics. It is helping to set higher standards in business practice and encouraging business men to conduct business by the Golden Rule; and that is not doing my cause any good."

A King receives vision from God, who then releases into the King's hands the resources or provision to accomplish the vision. Where there is provision, there is a King, since God truly desires resources to rest primarily in the hands of a King for the growing of His Kingdom, which happens to include the harvest of Matthew 9. This does not mean the people will not prosper or will be in poverty. It does mean that the King knows a certain amount of revenue will be generated by all other assignments to the vision, since they are part of the larger God-given vision he is to manifest. I have found that when I speak with leaders in the marketplace, many share the experience of God's divine intervention during a brief moment in time, where He poured the vision of building a community into them.

I remember teaching about entrepreneurs in a class one evening, and the Holy Spirit spoke to me concerning his divine impartation of vision to Kings. He shared how misaligned the Body of Christ has become when it comes to resources. The Holy Spirit revealed that God releases vision to his Kings, and then complementary ideas are put into other men to develop the marketplace and to call forth the involvement of others who play a role in manifesting the ideas. If an idea comes from God, and God is Spirit, then the idea is Spirit, and the gifts needed to accomplish this idea are also spiritual gifts. By spiritual gifts, I am referring to the functional gifts like leadership, compassion, craftsmanship, discernment, helps, administration, hospitality, and so on.

The Holy Spirit continued by revealing that the spiritual gifts inside of you are to connect with the vision and identify your particular assignment in bringing forth the vision. That is how God operates. When He releases an idea to you, the only reason He is releasing it to you is that He knows you carry the necessary gifts to manifest that idea. The idea comes from Him into you, and you are then supposed to call forth your gifts to bring forth that vision. Your ideas then call forth gifts from within others, and God's purpose and plan then manifests. There are many examples of this process as you look back throughout history.

Look at the story of Henry Ford, the man who first mass-produced the automobile. Henry Ford received the idea for the development of an automobile, and when he brought it forth, the vision brought forth the other gifts that were connected to create it. These ideas included everything from craftsmanship, administration, helps (customer service), teaching, writing, leadership and others. This created ripples of wealth in businesses that were created to accompany his vision. It created in America a culture that caused the nation to grow quicker as a result of being able to travel around faster.

Unfortunately, this very process of receiving ideas from Heaven and stepping out on the ideas is being blocked. This happens when we are fearful. We look at an idea as only being about and for *ourselves*.

We are frequently taught that our experience and education are solely what matters in the marketplace. That is not entirely true. God's way of doing things is not solely based on your education or experience, but is founded in your spiritual gifting. A King recognizes that this power does not come from control or manipulation, but by way of the authority he has been given to create an environment where those gifts are welcomed.

Unfortunately, many people are being led or influenced by *heathen* Kings. The only thing a heathen King desires is to build his own riches and wealth. This behavior is a joke; therefore, I refer to these heathen kings as "jokers." Jokers need to be replaced with real Kings, for our community will never grow under any other vision than one that is divinely given to the mind of a King. God gives Kings vision and then he brings men or women of God to help the King to fulfill that vision. All you have to do is read the Bible, both the Old and New Testament, and you will see that God gives vision to Kings. I know you have been told something other than this, but I challenge you to search it for yourself in the Word.

Abraham was a King in the marketplace. God made a covenant with him (Genesis 15) from which we all still benefit today. This covenant encompassed much more than material or financial wealth. When God saw that Abraham could be trusted with the material resources that he already possessed, He honored him and grew his resources to be even greater. I am speaking of both physical and spiritual growth that comes from a King using the resources for the glory of God and not the glory of men. A King understands that the resources are not only to accomplish something today, but also to see a return on the investment continually.

If you understand the capital markets, you will observe the way kings use resources. Kings use resources to invest in other ideas, businesses and markets, which in turn create an opportunity for jobs and many other contributions to a community.

If the resources were put into the hands of the priest, the people of Egypt would have died. In the same way, my people (Black Christians) are dying because the priests have spent the monies from the time of plenty and nothing is left for the famine.

The seven years of plenty that the land of Egypt had enjoyed came to an end, and the seven years of famine began, just as Joseph had said. There was famine in every other country, but there was food throughout Egypt. When the Egyptians began to be hungry, they cried out to the king for food. So he ordered them to go to Joseph and do what he told them. The famine grew worse and spread over the whole country, so Joseph opened all the storehouses and sold grain to the Egyptians. People came to Egypt from all over the world to buy grain from Joseph, because the famine was severe everywhere. (Genesis 41:53-56, GNB)

A Righteous King

Endow the king with your justice, O God,
    the royal son with your righteousness.
May he judge your people in righteousness,
    your afflicted ones with justice.
May the mountains bring prosperity to the people,
    the hills the fruit of righteousness.
May he defend the afflicted among the people
    and save the children of the needy;
      may he crush the oppressor.
May he endure as long as the sun,
    as long as the moon, through all generations.
May he be like rain falling on a mown field,
    like showers watering the earth.
In his days may the righteous flourish
    and prosperity abound till the moon is no more.

> *May he rule from sea to sea*
> *and from the River to the ends of the earth.*
> *May the desert tribes bow before him*
> *and his enemies lick the dust.*
> *May the kings of Tarshish and of distant shores*
> *bring tribute to him.*
> *May the kings of Sheba and Seba*
> *present him gifts.*
> *May all kings bow down to him*
> *and all nations serve him.* (Psalms 72:1-1, NIV)

We first must understand there is none righteous. "Why do you ask me about what is good?" Jesus replied. "There is only One who is good. If you want to enter life, keep the commandments." (Matthew 19:17, NIV)

A King must have godly counsel and moral clarity from someone he can trust and who has his best interest at heart. It takes a righteous priest to walk alongside a King in order to keep a King obedient to the operating manual (Holy Bible) and upstanding.

The impact a righteous King will have on a kingdom is beyond comprehension to most of us. A King with a heart for the things of God will create an environment where integrity is more important than short-term profit. The elevation of those with godly character is what a righteous King desires at his table. How does a King learn to stay away from the many satanic traps that sit waiting for his weak moments to capture him into a web of sin? A King must seek to have a righteous priest and a prophet that hears the voice of God to provide future revelation needed to make current decisions as a part of his inner circle.

When the righteous are in authority, the people rejoice: but when the wicked beareth rule, the people mourn. (Proverbs 29:2, KJV)

A King who desires to lead righteously must be willing to sort through the swindlers who hang around counterfeiting as priests with the singular agenda of getting to a King's resources. The sad truth is that very few prophets understand that their role is to walk with the King in order to provide the godly compass needed in the daily decisions of a kingdom.

If a King rules from a godly Kingdom perspective, then he will always fund the priest as well as the work of the kingdom. By the way, the work of the kingdom is more in the marketplace than in any worship center. A King understands the importance of sowing into true Kingdom work, since he benefits from the impact it has on the people he governs. Kings will provide grants, foundations and support for many organizations working towards the greater good of the people. Go into any museum, cultural center, university, hospital, clinic, rehabilitation center, and you will see their names on the wall. They donate and influence the areas they lord over, as well as work with other kings to have a larger impact in the area in which they rule.

The impact of a King throughout the marketplace makes a church denomination look small—that is, if you equate Kingdom work to nothing more than a conference speaking engagement, a new building or a pastor's wealth. I challenge you to read the stories of Christian business owners like Truett Cathy, the founder of Chic-fil-A, and Sam Walton, the founder of Wal-Mart. You will see the direct correlation between a righteous King and the impact he has on the local, national and global marketplace. The impact that Mr. Cathy, for example, has on all communities where his restaurants operate, as well as the many other works Chic-fil-A is doing around the world, is nothing short of amazing.

You will find that righteous Kings will have a righteous priest walking beside them for guidance and to declare what the Word of God says concerning their daily leading. Truett Cathy operates under a King's mantle, but rules by God's Kingdom principles. The impact of Mr. Cathy and Chick-Fil-A was probably due to his walk with his shepherd, who directed him to the Father. Mr. Cathy had to come into a relationship with God that allowed him to lead his kingdom by the will of God.

The manner in which a King might choose to change the world is a very serious business. Further, such power in the hands of a corrupt King could create a true tyranny. King David of Israel is an example of a righteous King whose heart was for his God and his people.

When the King has No Priest

As I mentioned before, the relationship between the King and priest is one of God-ordained interdependence. They need each other's gifts and ministry offerings in order for the Kingdom of God to work in its proper order. In recent years, we have seen the evidence of many Kings who have no one walking with them closely to help them operate with God's will in mind. I would dare say that many of these unrighteous Kings attend some worship center, but have no shepherd walking with them.

A righteous King creates an environment where others can walk into their vision, and their vision is welcomed. When a King is corrupt and his kingdom falls, those who are trying to come up and better themselves fall, too. You have to be able to identify a King, not only by what he likes around him, but also by what he does.

I have personally experienced how easy it is to become corrupt in your own pride and selfish desires when operating as a King in the marketplace. A King needs a righteous priest to be concerned about the state of his soul, mind and spirit and to help him walk in the righteousness of Christ. If he hears the heart of the priest concerning his kingdom, he will ask the priest to meet with him to gain insight, prophecy and instruction, and also so he can support the priest's role with the people in the kingdom.

The following words that Paul gave to Timothy are something that the average King without a priest will never know. This instruction was never given to me until I began to study the Word of God for myself. As I look back on my own past ignorance, I pray other Kings come into contact with true priests who are willing to provide counsel like this.

> *Command those who are rich in the present world not to be arrogant nor to put their hope in wealth, which is so uncertain, but to put their hope in God, who richly provides us with everything for our enjoyment. Command them to do good, to be rich in good deeds, and to be generous and willing to communicate. In this way they will lay up treasure for themselves as a firm foundation for the coming age, so that they may take hold of the life that is truly life.*
> (1 Timothy 6:17-19, NIV)

I recommend all marketplace leaders connect with organizations like FCCI, CBMC, C12, Corporate Chaplains and others due to the importance of having a priest in your place of work. The gift of having a priest connected to your business is critical to the steering of your team in the ways of God when distractions come to move you off course.

A Corrupt King

Unfortunately, I have found that the most successful marketplace Kings are often the most spiritually immature or appeased. Some of us have seen greed, selfish ambitions, lusts, division and manipulation rule the marketplace for so long. A King who rules with a heart for God seems almost non-existent.

A corrupt King will always be focused only on his agenda. You can see an example in the movie *Troy*. King Agamemnon, who ruled over the people, wanted to grow his kingdom, and he could have cared less about how many soldiers had to die to do it. Obsessed with his quest to conquer, Agamemnon only concerned his mind with—and became consumed by—acquiring more money, influence and resources. His motive was no longer a vision that includes a kingdom, but it is now distorted by a vision that includes him having more wealth.

You can identify a corrupt King by his words. A corrupt King often says things that vaunt him as the brand and the business. Everything around him bears *his* name. When he thinks he *is* the brand, the brand is his own name. That is why some kings put their name on everything. He is the brand. He is the business. When you are around him, you notice immediately that it is really about him and his ego.

A true King understands that he is not the business nor is he the brand. Nor does he desire to be, as that would mean that the business would rise or fall with his identity. This would remove his ability to delegate authority and hold people accountable. When it is all about him, the very people to whom authority should be delegated to accomplish the vision now cannot be held accountable to it. A corrupt King sometimes goes even further. In the story of Sparta, in the time of King Leonidas, Sparta was famed for its war-mongering and its ruthlessly efficient military. King Leonidas of Sparta encountered the all-powerful King Xerxes, who ruled over the vast dominion of Persia. Xerxes had given himself the title "King of Kings" and had even claimed divinity—and he required his subjects to treat him accordingly. He wanted to be carried in a litter and ushered in on a platform with his servants all around him. In the story, he tells Leonidas that he is willing to *kill* any of his men if they do not carry out his instructions to the letter. Leonidas flips it. He retorts that he would be willing to *die* for any of his men.

A corrupt King is not willing to sacrifice for the overall good. He is willing to say that the *people* of the kingdom may have to come together to sacrifice for the greater good of the kingdom. In Matthew 23, Jesus is speaking on that type of leader. He warns that they will put the burdens around your neck and will carry nothing. That is what a corrupt King does.

A corrupt King oppresses a kingdom or community. He uses the people, so he can collect more "taxes." He then uses the money to buy objects for himself or to order more work to be done. You can tell when the King is corrupt when his people struggle and fall. The crumbling of a kingdom is even greater when a corrupt King is at the helm, for the whole kingdom goes down. The only hope to restore such a crumbled kingdom is a King operating from the mindset of compassion and reformation. I don't have to look farther than the city—Detroit, MI—in which I lived for a year, to see the debilitating results of this dynamic.

Everybody fails when a King is corrupt. Look at the economic system over the last couple of years in the United States as well as other countries. The fall occurred under the rule of corrupt Kings, and now the entire nation is being punished. The ones who are trying to pull themselves up have fallen because corrupt Kings were running the show.

Another present-day example of what happens when corrupt Kings are in control occurred in New York, the financial center of this country. It is no coincidence that a survey conducted in 1998 revealed that fewer than 1% of people in Manhattan said they believed in God. Yet 70% of all business owners, 50% of politicians, 3% in the arts and entertainment and 2% in media outside of Manhattan believe in God. It is imperative that the Kings, who are movers and shakers, remain uncorrupted, so they can operate with high ethics and integrity.

A corrupt King "pimps" the people. He exploits their weaknesses, not only to bring in money for him and his heirs, but also any other commodity he might desire, even casual sex. He knows how to use his position of power in the community to set up or buy into prostitution, casinos, and gentlemen's clubs to increase his wealth. These systems and venues bring in plenty of money quickly, but of course they pervert the people, suck the kingdom dry and kill the community. Consider the "success" of Vegas or Atlantic City, where ordinary people survive by serving the needs of tourists who come to enjoy ungodly entertainment. The visitors come into the casino to gamble, shop and to have sex with prostitutes, and then they leave. The ordinary employees do not prosper. The money sits in the hand of the King, while the whole kingdom suffers.

A corrupt King will allow these immoral visions to flourish in his kingdom. It is still a vision, but it is immoral. Whose role is it to protect the community from immorality being pushed in the market? It is the King's. The King could have prevented them from coming in by saying, "No!" Kings could easily remove the immoral television shows that dominate the listings by removing their advertising support.

A corrupt King's greed, pride, desire to gratify himself and take credit or glory for his success will lead him to failure. This failure will not only be monetary, but also in the areas of his family, children, relationships, leadership effectiveness and reputation. A King is always looking for clarity from those he can trust, for there is no greater isolation and loneliness than that of a true King.

Do you want an inside view of how a corrupt King operates? Watch the TV shows *American Gangster* or *American Greed*, which give a history of the criminal activity of both individuals and gangs. I don't think they could ever run out of material to do that show. Everyone who enters the gangster's orbit, both the police and his minions, say that he is a genius. They admire the systems, processes, procedures, and organization that he put in place, as well as the resources that came to him. *American Gangster* shows a community of Kings with no direction. Look at Frank Lucas, Lucky Luciano, and Al Capone, and you will recognize the model. You will see how the enemy takes a King and corrupts him to the dismay of the community.

American Gangster exposes the mind of a King who has not been put into an environment or a culture that will encourage his gifts or allow him to grow. I can name many men who started something unrighteous at a young age and it grew throughout the world, as Tookie Williams did with the gang the Crips. The Bloods gang was started as a faction of the Crips, which are both now worldwide organizations.

Another area that we need to be aware of and that leads to corruption is the spirit of being self-made. The world likes to imply that our financial success is somehow self-made, which in turn feeds into our ego. Ask the Father to deliver you from the perversion of being a self-made success.

Kings are the Gatekeepers

> *During the time Mordecai was sitting at the king's gate, Bigthana and Teresh, two of the king's officers who guarded the doorway, became angry and conspired to assassinate King Xerxes.* (Esther 2:21, NIV)

The kingdoms of old times had walls built around them. The King's vision included walls. These walls not only protected the citizens from outsiders, they also protected people outside the walls from being influenced by his kingdom. Those walls were there for both internal and external protection. When people saw the walls, they knew they were inside this kingdom. A citizen could look up from his daily activities, see the walls and recognize that he was in a particular kingdom, operating under certain laws. An outsider might also see the walls in the distance and realize there is a kingdom, and it must have a King. The kingdom is a designated territory under some principality or power, which can be both physical and spiritual.

When the King is the gatekeeper, he is announcing that he has been given authority to rule over a specific territory. He starts with his home. The walls tell everyone, "This is where my kingdom ends. Outside the walls is not my concern. But inside these walls, I am responsible." The walls delineate the area under the King's protection. Usually, the only way anyone could enter within his walls was through the gate. The gate was guarded all day and locked down at nightfall, since under the cover of darkness was usually when the enemy tried to invade.

The role of the King is to understand that there are some things that can undermine the kingdom or community.

When the President of the United States is sworn in, he is sworn to protect the United States from enemies domestic and abroad. The domestic enemy is the one who does not want to adhere to the laws of the land. The president is sworn to protect the citizens from those individuals who may undermine the kingdom by ignoring the laws and doing things their own way. The president has the right to, and is sworn

to, protect us from that. He is also sworn as a gatekeeper who delegates authority to the Department of
Defense, including the FBI, the CIA, the local police
and all of those such entities.

There are some things that can undermine the
kingdom or community inside a home. A King should
first of all be King of his own home. Since a man is
the "King" of his home, his home should represent his
vision. If he is a Christian who represents the Kingdom
vision in his home, the kingdom within his home
is the product. If his home is not modeled in alignment with the original franchise (Jesus and the Word
made visible), then roles and responsibilities could
easily become misaligned. In some homes, the man
is removed altogether, and the home is completely
undermined. In such a case, all other roles become less
potent. The franchise of the family is no longer operating at its optimal and intended level. You will notice
men becoming the homemaker and doing the traditional female role of the home. The female begins to
take on the traditional male responsibilities, while both
are undermining the true nature of their roles. Once
functional roles in the home have become less clear,
then Satan has you on the ropes and is ready to knock
you out.

So that I am clear, please understand the Kings are
the ones used to affect culture. Media, business, education, family, politics, entertainment and all other indus-
tries are influenced by Kings. If the King allows himself
to be influenced by Satan, he will use his influence for

Satan's agenda. The battles waged in the land are a direct reflection of the Kings. Companies like Apple, Starbucks, Target and others are heavily influenced by men who do not have God's agenda on their minds. If you look at their logos and what side of the issues they are taking, you will see for yourself. What is happening behind closed doors is Kings joining forces in groups like the Illuminati, skull and bones, free masons and others. I strongly advise you to consider the method by which society is being influenced in many Satanic ways and consider the people behind the movement.

The gates are open to immoral and destructive spirits designed to destroy the very moral fabric of our society. We must have Christian Kings come together to rebuke these spirits and release the ways of the Kingdom of God. Kings arise!

CHAPTER THREE

The Priest

What is the Biblical Role of a Pastor?

T he pastor is ordained of God to ensure that the sheep of God know and operate in the ways of God. The sheep include the Kings God has placed within his flock. Anyone who is called to operate in the five-fold ministry, as an Apostle, Prophet, Pastor, Evangelist, or Teacher of the Word of God, is also considered a priest. In fulfilling this commission, a priest is to keep himself clean in all aspects of his life, to spend time in the presence of the Lord, and to help equip the sheep in the manifestation of the Kingdom of God.

I asked the question, "What is the role of a pastor?" to the more than thirty pastors who were present at one of my Tuesday morning Bible Study that I facilitate. To my surprise, not one of them said to shepherd or equip the sheep.

I wish this were not true because it would make it less necessary and more challenging for me to write this book. But this is the fact: not one pastor in the room understood that his primary role was to equip or shepherd the sheep. Worse, this mindset is not limited to those pastors who were there that morning. This lack of understanding permeates the Body of Christ all over the country.

The instruction provided in God's word tells me that as part of the five-fold ministry, pastors are to help equip the sheep for the work of their ministry. The pastor is not assigned a territory to rule (except in his own home). His role, along with that of the elders, is to tend to the sheep that belong to the Master—the Father through Christ Jesus. As I evaluate pastors on the Word of God, then I must question why so many have revealed to me that they feel their role is not about the sheep but all about themselves or their ministries.

Ephesians 4:11 (NIV) states:

> *And He Himself gave some to be apostles, some prophets, some evangelists, and some pastors and teachers, for the equipping of the saints for the work of ministry, for the edifying of the Body of Christ, till we all come to the unity of the faith and the knowledge of the Son of God, to a perfect Man, to the measure of the statue of the fullness of Christ.*

The pastor and all who are called to the five-fold ministry play an equally crucial role in the equipping of the Body of Christ. Knowing this, why is it that the pastor is popularly considered to be the head honcho, the number one influencer, and in many cases, the richest person in the congregation? This is not scriptural; it is a deceptive and controlling spirit from demonic influences. The question I most often ask the Father is, "Why are the people silent and allowing this to happen?"

In order to break this demonic influence fully, we have to examine a priest's (pastor's) role in the land carefully. The pastor is to operate as the shepherd of the sheep, directing them to the Master. The only way the Body of Christ can be directed to the Father is by way of the Son, Jesus Christ. A pastor is to *equip* the people with the tools of God to make the Kingdom visible in all areas of their lives. However, today's pastors spend far too much time *preaching* at the people. There is a difference between teaching and preaching.

Teaching is the process of sharing the truth of the Word of God to show or help a person learn how to do something through knowledge and insight. Teaching is bringing the truth of God to believers. It does not need highly emotional and dramatic presentation to convince the people. The Word stands on its own power.

Preaching is the passionate, emotional and sometimes dramatic presentation that is required to grab the attention of unbelievers and lead them into the teaching of the Truth of the Word. When Jesus told

His disciples to go preach the gospel, he was sending them out to those who were not yet believers. I believe the gospel to be the birth, life, death, resurrection and second coming of Jesus Christ.

Preaching is not required in the true equipping of sheep. To preach the good news of Jesus Christ is the role of all believers. Preaching is not a part of the five-fold ministry. The Lord made some apostles, prophets, evangelists, teachers, and some pastors, not preachers.

Yet a vast number of pastors continually preach at the sheep. They never truly teach or equip them to do the work of the Kingdom of God. If a community is led by those who are called "preachers," then that community is not truly being equipped.

In doing my research for this work, I came across a great teaching of truth on the role of the Biblical Pastor. I read a bit of an article titled [1]*What is the biblical role of a pastor in a church?* written by Craig Bluemel, a Biblical Pastor who spent his life raising up and equipping other Biblical Pastors. He clearly explains the role of the Pastor based on scripture:

> The office of a pastor in the Christian church has been a role that has been accepted without question over the past 400+ years. Since the days of John Calvin, who emerged in church leadership in the 1500's, church government has consisted of the pastor and

---

1 Bluemel, Craig. "What is the biblical role of a pastor in a church?" http://www.bibleanswerstand.org/pastors.htm

the elders, who are elected representatives of the congregation. This governmental structure is almost exclusively pyramid in nature with the pastor as the head and the elder board beneath him. This is clearly in conflict with the teachings of the New Testament, as I will prove.

The Greek work for pastor is *poimen*. The literal meaning of the word *poimen* is shepherd. English translations of the Bible only translate *poimen* as "pastor" only one time in the entire New Testament in Ephesians 4:11 (NASB):

And He gave some as apostles, and some as prophets, and some as evangelists, and some as pastors and teachers…

Here pastor is listed as one of the God-appointed offices in the church, but it is plural "pastors" and rules of Greek grammar demand that pastors and teachers here refer to one office. So if we accurately translate *poimen* to be shepherds, and it is one office, more properly Ephesians 4:11 reads "shepherds as teachers." The Greek word *poimen* is translated as "shepherd" 17 times in the New Testament; below are its various uses:

- Four times it is used of literal shepherds caring for literal sheep;

- Eight times it refers to Jesus as the Great Shepherd of the church;

- Four times it refers to leadership of true believers, as either true or false leaders;

- One time it is used of an office in the church.

The shepherds must be a plurality to prevent the aforementioned abuses from destroying the church. Today's church with its one-man leadership not only fails to meet the needs of the individual believer who can never spend quality time with overloaded pastors, but it also puts those pastors in a position of vulnerability to demonic deception.

The article continues in outlining how to regain the intended order of God in the five-fold ministry and church according to Scriptural principles. The article's teachings are continued in the last chapter of this book, *Restoring the Order of the King and Priest.*

A true shepherd does not leave his fingerprints on those whom God has ordained him to equip. A shepherd is to guide and nudge the sheep in the direction God wants them to go. If he has left his fingerprints on the sheep, then he has pushed too hard and attempted to control the sheep by force or manipulation.

The Character of a Priest

A priest is to live a holy and upright life. This is critical, since it is his role to keep the sheep of God clean in their heart and spirit. It is impossible for a priest to complete this assignment if he is not clean in his heart and spirit. Priests are to guide the believers of the Lord into becoming perfected in Christ—becoming without spot or wrinkle while they are here upon the earth (see Ephesians 5:27).

A priest or someone who is called to operate in the five-fold ministry is to serve as a beacon of light to others. He is to live in a way that does not contradict the Word of God as the truth. He is to live a consecrated and sanctified life that sets him apart, not by his words or having to preach to the people, but by the way he lives.

A true priest or one who moves in the five-fold ministry is to live by the same standards that the Word has outlined by which an elder or deacon is to live.

> *Here is a trustworthy saying: Whoever aspires to be an overseer desires a noble task. Now the overseer is to be above reproach, faithful to his wife, temperate, self-controlled, respectable, hospitable, able to teach, not given to drunkenness, not violent but gentle, not quarrelsome, not a lover of money. He must manage his own family well and see that his children obey him, and he must do so in a manner worthy of full respect. (If anyone does not know how*

to manage his own family, how can he take care of God's church?) He must not be a recent convert, or he may become conceited and fall under the same judgment as the devil. He must also have a good reputation with outsiders, so that he will not fall into disgrace and into the devil's trap.

In the same way, deacons are to be worthy of respect, sincere, not indulging in much wine, and not pursuing dishonest gain. They must keep hold of the deep truths of the faith with a clear conscience. They must first be tested; and then if there is nothing against them, let them serve as deacons. In the same way, the women are to be worthy of respect, not malicious talkers but temperate and trustworthy in everything. A deacon must be faithful to his wife and must manage his children and his household well. Those who have served well gain an excellent standing and great assurance in their faith in Christ Jesus. (1 Timothy 3:1-13, NIV)

The priest is not someone perfect who should be held to the level of Christ, but respected for the calling on his life. We need to be very careful to make sure the church has the checks and balances in place to make sure these principles are followed. It is no longer acceptable to have pastors embezzle, fornicate, commit adultery, lie and steal, while we remain loyal to his gifts and position without accountability.

I thank God for the many pastors who work hard to hold to these truths and repent when they fall short. We continue to pray for you daily.

The Authority of a Priest

Just as all believers should walk in their full authority over all things in both the spiritual and natural realm, a priest should have a clear understanding of this authority, so he can stand in the gap for his flock as they learn how to move in their full authority. A priest has authority over those whom God has assigned to him—his flock. A priest has been granted the authority to speak life into their lives and guide them in the ways of the Lord.

A priest has divine authority to enter the throne of God and receive direction from the Lord on behalf of his flock and of the King(s) to whom he has been assigned. He has the authority to identify and teach his flock how to recognize and move in their gifts from God. The priest has also been given authority from the Lord to disciple his flock and provide correction when they are off track or operating outside of God's righteousness.

A priest, under the New Testament, is not to come between man and God, but is to lead the sheep to be able to hear from the Holy Spirit themselves. He does not have the authority to control or coerce the people of God. He should be raising up the flock in their gifts and the teachings of the Gospel, so they are fully equipped to go out and apply their teachings to the marketplace.

The priest has been given the authority to keep the hearts and spirits of the people of God clean and pure through the blood of Jesus Christ. Just as the priests of the Old Testament stood at the door of the tabernacle where the congregation entered and oversaw the altar of burnt offering that represented atonement for their unclean behavior, the priest of the New Testament has been granted the authority to oversee the purification of the hearts of the sheep and make sure their spirits are cleansed, so they are granted access to the inheritance of the Kingdom of God (see Galatians 5:15–21).

A priest who is called to operate in the role of an apostle is responsible for overseeing other priests to make sure they are fully submitted to the teachings of Christ. It is imperative that those who carry this role take back the role of correction in the worship center boldly. These apostolic priests should collect monthly reports, not just of how many members showed up for service, but especially of how many signs, wonders and miracles manifested, how many were healed, how many were delivered and how many accepted Christ as their Lord and Savior. It is the apostle's responsibility to train up and send out ministries into the marketplace to truly bring light to the people. This number should also be tracked on a monthly basis and given in a report of the state of their flock. Each of these numbers should be more important than how much offering the worship center brought in and how many people came through the door.

The Influence of the Priest

The influence of a priest should be evident in the fruit his sheep are producing in their lives. If a priest is properly shepherding the people of God, the sheep should be experiencing life—and life more abundantly in all areas. They should have health in their physical bodies. They should be fulfilling the call of the Lord. The people of God should be examples of the power and authority of Christ everywhere they go.

Just as the influence of a King should be evident in the results he produces through the people, the influence of a priest should operate in the same way. This influence should be evident in those whom a priest disciples as followers of Jesus Christ. In addition, a priest's teaching of the truth should always be followed by signs and wonders (see Mark 16:17).

The Mindset of a Priest

The mindset of a priest should be geared completely toward the perfection of the saints for the work of the ministry and the edification of the Body of Christ. He is focused first on experiencing the heart of God in his life and then feeding the sheep with knowledge and understanding of the ways of the Lord. This includes how to walk in divine authority and becoming a vessel for the greater works of Jesus (see John 14:12).

The mindset of a priest should be all about seeing the Body of Christ heal itself in all aspects. A priest should not be able to tolerate someone in his flock living beneath the promises of the Word of God. He should be identifying and developing the gifts of the sheep, so they can operate effectively in the marketplace. Everything the priest thinks about should create teachings and instruction on how to understand the Word of God and operate in its statutes and precepts.

A true priest's focus is on empowerment of God's sheep, so they can operate in the full measure of Christ. He should concentrate entirely on people being whole in all areas of their lives and moving in the full manifestation of their salvation, which includes being whole, healed, delivered, set free, safe and sound from harm. He should train the people up in taking their authority over the adversary in all areas of their lives, so they live victorious lives and not the victimized, pitiful lives most Christians live today.

The Language of a Priest

The role of a priest is to hear from God clearly and share what he hears verbatim. Therefore, his language sounds very different from that of a King. The priest's language should be filled with the certainty, authority, dominion and power of Christ. While part of the priest's role is to be compassionate toward the sheep of the Lord, he is to raise the standard by which the sheep are living and be able to communicate this standard clearly and without hesitation.

A priest should understand enough about the marketplace to be able to engage a King in conversation that reflects that understanding. This conversation must be beyond stereotypical jargon. He should be producing good fruit and should reply with Holy Spirit-inspired language that will resonate with the King.

A priest should be recognized more by what he does not say than by what he does say. He should listen more than he speaks, so he can hear the voice of God in all situations to provide proper counsel and advice to his flock, including the King(s) the Lord has assigned to him (see James 1:9). The priest will walk along with the King to declare what the Lord is saying to the people and to the King. A priest cannot decree a plan in the land—only a King can, with the spiritual guidance of the righteous priest.

The Priest and King-Melchizedek

The double anointing of priest and King is very rare. I strongly believe that Christians are called to be both spiritual Kings with authority to rule and priests with authority to declare the Word of the Lord. The Word of God states this in Revelation 1:16 (KJV):

> *And (He) hath made us **Kings** and **Priests** unto God and His Father; to Him be glory and dominion forever and ever. Amen.*

Jesus impacts the disciples from a priestly stand-point, but He teaches to them from a marketplace perspective. He is showing them God's way of doing things as a priest, but is encouraging them to go out into the marketplace. This is how someone with the double anointing of King and priest operates.

There are some people who carry an anointing in both areas, as a marketplace King and a shepherd of God's sheep. But it is very rare. Examples of pastors who carry this double anointing are Bill Hybels, A. R. Bernard, Bill Winston, Floyd Flake and Kirbyjon Caldwell. (I do not speak on the character of these men, since I do not know them personally.) They are anointed in both marketplace and worship center leadership. We have seen so few examples of someone who carries this double anointing that it's possible you may never have met one. I shall include a few notes about Kirbyjon Caldwell, an example of a pastor who carries the double anointing.

In reading the [2]biography of Mr. Caldwell, I noticed how God developed this man in the marketplace before calling him into the role of priest.

> Although he was very successful financially through marketplace accomplishments, Caldwell felt called to Christian ministry and subsequently attended the Perkins School of Theology at Southern Methodist University, receiving his masters in Divinity in 1981. While completing his degree, Caldwell was appointed Associate Pastor at St. Mary's United Methodist Church in Houston.
>
> One of the major themes of Caldwell's preaching has been the need for his congregation to follow Jesus Christ's lead by being

---

2 www.kingdombuilders.com/pastor-kirbyjon-caldwell

actively involved in community service. Taking the lead, Caldwell has transformed the Windsor Village United Methodist Church into an all-purpose community help center. Nonprofit organizations organized by the church include: Patrice House, a shelter for abused children; a tutoring program for schoolchildren; and a program that matches teens to mentors.

Windsor Village United Methodist Church had 7,000 members by 1994 and 11,000 by 1996.

To accommodate the size of the congregation, in 1993, the church purchased a former Kmart in one of the most blighted parts of Houston and renovated it into the Power Center (a play on the retailing term "power center"). In addition to worship space, the Power Center includes a school, a medical clinic, satellite classrooms for a local community college, low-cost office space, a branch of the Texas Commerce Bank (there were previously no banks in the entire neighborhood), as well as charities such as a Women, Infants, and Children nutrition program, and an AIDS outreach center. The mission of the Power Center is to create jobs in the low-income neighborhood and to teach members of the neighborhood how to create wealth. The Center's motto is from Isaiah

61.4: "They shall repair the ruined cities and restore what has long lain desolate."

Unlike many churches, no one sits on the stage during services, including Mr. Kirbyjon Caldwell.

I have never met Mr. Caldwell, but the more I read his story and impact in the marketplace since becoming a pastor, the more I see what true leadership looks like when someone carries a double anointing in worship center and marketplace.

A marketplace King will easily submit to this kind of shepherd. He has been tested and has been proven to understand the marketplace successfully as a King. The same effectiveness is shown in his role as a shepherd. If I were called to be a shepherd of God's sheep and needed a mentor, I would run to Mr. Caldwell. I recommend you read his book, *The Gospel of Good Success: A Road Map to Spiritual, Emotional, and Financial Wholeness.*

Do not make the mistake of trying to be both if you do not carry a double anointing of King and priest. If you are motivated by the size of the congregation, the number of church events, financial gain, community influence or any reason other than you believe you are anointed in both areas—you do not carry this double anointing. Your heart must be in the right place, which is for the Kingdom of God to be revealed.

Those who carry this double anointing usually come from the marketplace as a King. I'm not talking about a manager or an administrator of a company. The worst mistake you can make is to assume that someone who manages a company or works for the government necessarily has a King's mind..

When a King comes from owning or having influence in the marketplace and then receives the calling in the form of a pastorate, you will find that the sheep or community grows immensely. This King's mind is like that of David, who was both King and priest. David had the mind of a King to take over, to do battle, to conquer, but he also had the heart of God to declare, "Thus saith the Lord." King-priests are very few and far between. You can identify them when they operate as both King and priest by the way their whole community grows—and it is not determined by a worship center! These men have already built entire communities.

The Culture of Pastors who have Forgotten their Priesthood

Let's talk about the culture of the pastors who do not understand their priesthood. I can speak to this from my connections with many pastors, which have given me firsthand knowledge of the lack of leadership many of them exhibit.

These pastors hang out together, limit their communication to others in their pastor circles, and repeatedly speak at one another's conferences. These pastors can easily be identified by the way they never have an original Word from the Lord. They all sound too much alike when they speak at each other's worship centers and events.

These pastors see their ministry as their family business and usually put their family members on payroll. You will find the attempt to pass the ministry to their children, to pass down the control. This is very similar to the model of the slave master and business leaders. The slave master and business owner has the right to desire to pass the business and assets to their children; however, the pastor does not. The gift of pastor is determined by God and is not specific to an inheritance. Be wary of spouses being given titles of co-pastors and children being made employees or leaders of particular ministries.

I have noticed that when you sit with some pastors, anywhere in the country, they will show you their building plans, share how the number of church members has grown over the years and what their membership numbers are now. They tell you about their beach houses, their cars, their homes and how much they have accumulated for themselves. Almost without fail, they are telling you this while sitting in an elaborate office located in a nice worship center. Many of them dare say that they are not responsible for what is happening in the neighborhoods of the worship centers they oversee. This is a pastor who has forgotten his priesthood, and this train of thought is contributing to the state of our churches and community. Warning: The next step for these lost pastors will be to become gurus, book promoters and motivational speakers. This movement is of Satan and it denies the true power of the gospel of Jesus Christ as well as the role of a pastor.

Kings and Priests Walking Together

A King must keep near him a priest who will help him to govern with a biblical viewpoint and a righteous influence. The only way this will happen is if a priest walks alongside the King, understanding his role of declaring "thus says the Lord," so the King can make decisions that are righteous in nature, and the people in the kingdom will benefit.

I use the example of King Darius, who "decreed in the land" in Daniel chapter 6. This is very important for us to know, since the only one who can decree laws in the land is *the King*. If you think back on the many press conferences over the years where a King in the marketplace has gotten into trouble, he usually goes running for a pastor to not only give him advice, but also to stand with him in the eyes of the public.

It unfortunately happens that the only reason why some pastors stand with a King at this time is due to the potential outlay of resources that a bewildered King will release during this vulnerable time. My question is, "Where was the priest before the King fell?" When all things are operating in proper order, the priest is on guard to keep the King equipped and guided spiritually, so some of these falls are avoided. We have seen the outcomes when this doesn't happen.

The Word is very clear about how the Lord will treat pastors who are corrupt and who have not properly equipped the people of God to operate effectively in their lives. The Lord says:

> *Woe be unto the pastors that destroy and scatter the sheep of my pasture! saith the LORD. Therefore thus saith the LORD God of Israel against the pastors that feed my people; Ye have scattered my flock, and driven them away, and have not visited them: behold, I will visit upon you the evil of your doings, saith the LORD.*
> (Jeremiah 23:1, KJV)

It is true that most pastors are doing the best they can to walk morally and under authority; however, too many are falling prey to corruption, greed, fornication, adultery, manipulation and spiritual heresy. We must be aware that the corruption is not only growing but is unrestrained. Sexual perversion is now becoming the predominate method of manipulation and possession. Please open your eyes to what is happening, especially in the African-American community.

However, when Kings and priests walk together, according to God's ordained order, miracles happen in transforming our communities, our churches become a hub of spiritual support and the resource it was intended to be, and the Body of Christ affects the world as predestined.

Priests are Not the Gatekeepers of the Community

As a disciple, you are a gatekeeper, which not only means keeping others on the outside, but letting some others in. That is what the gatekeeper is all about.

Where there are gatekeepers, there is little to no crime. Where there are gatekeepers, the kingdom grows and other people want to live in that kingdom.

For example, the Raleigh-Durham area grew when Kings came together and agreed that this kingdom would be one in which people with ideas could enter. As a result, Research Triangle was established, and many corporations entered. When that kind of activity is welcomed, the kingdom grows.

Many of our African-American church communities have no such gatekeepers, and the lack of growth is evident.

The opposite can happen in an area that is controlled by priests. In that same city—where people are thriving, growing, bringing their ideas from out west and north, wanting to live in this community and coming here to retire—some people can be under bondage to their priests. In such a case, a wall exists *within* the city. What is separating them? It is that a wall was built by priests, so they could control what they think is their kingdom, as if they personally own a section of the same city.

If the sheep could only pass outside this wall, they would see that they live in the land of milk and honey. But no, a corrupt priest will not allow that. He knows that if he exposes the sheep to freedom, he will no longer be able to manipulate them. Priests should be gatekeepers of the pasture—but not of the whole community. They should absolutely be impacting the community in positive ways, but not gatekeeping. When a priest attempts to operate as gatekeeper for the whole city, you know he is corrupt. And I see this in almost every city. A true King as community gatekeeper is a completely different story. Kings will use their influence to allow for organizations and resources to help the people—things like family centers, drug-clinics, parks, cultural development and others to create a wholesome life for the people. These Kings will work together for the good of the community because they value what others bring to the table.

Who is your gatekeeper? If it is a priest, then he is not supposed to be controlling you by preventing you from going outside the church walls. What he is actually supposed to be protecting you from is straying outside of the Kingdom of God. The gate between the church and the world is actually a gate through which the sheep are supposed to be sent. Jesus kept commanding His disciples to go out to the lost, so doing that never removes you from the Kingdom of God. Jesus taught that when you go to the lost say, "The Kingdom of Heaven is at hand!"

The shepherd is supposed to teach the sheep of God how to operate in the Kingdom of God and how to take the Kingdom to the lost. He is not supposed to keep them confined in a building. Your purpose is to go out and represent the Kingdom of God, which is not by territory, not by land, but to be sent out to the lost and declare to them another way. Whenever a priest claims he has used the building to "protect" the sheep, it is deceptive. He is not using it to protect them; he is using it to control them. It is the same for an overbearing parent who keeps his children locked up in the home. The Kingdom of God, for which they are supposed to be Ambassadors, is not ever in a building; it is within them. You *are* the territory of the Kingdom of God.

> *Do you not know that your bodies are temples of the Holy Spirit, Who is in you, Whom you have received from God?* (1 Corinthians 6:19, NIV)

The territory of the Kingdom of God is the person who carries God the Holy Spirit inside him. John 15:10 (NIV) refers to this when Jesus says:

> *"If you keep my commands, you will remain in My love, just as I have kept My Father's commands and remain in His love."*

These over-controlling gatekeepers are preventing the passage of the very people who are supposed to represent the Kingdom of Heaven to the lost. They stand at the gate saying they don't want you to exit. How will the lost know Christ as their Savior unless you go out among the people?

The wolves have been invited into the pasture of the Black church with his claim of sowing seeds into their ministries. These wolves use television stations directed at minorities so to drain them dry of their finances with a promise of future gain. The gates are open to those claiming that "money cometh" while taking huge offerings from the congregants and using the funds to purchase their personal material goods.

When I was a child, I remember a New York pastor coming to my small town for a week to conduct a revival. The pastor came in a long stretch limousine with ten or more assistants who wiped his sweat from his brow. The community was in awe as if God himself had come to their territory. What was amazing is how many offerings were taken during the week and how nothing was invested into the people. The gatekeepers let the wolf come into the community to drain the people, and I am sure they divided the spoils between the New York and local pastor.

I sit on some boards of directors and places of influence with Kings, and I have noticed a particular pattern when it comes to support for the African-American community. This pattern is that whenever you want to provide for the needs of the African-American community, you must go through the pastors. This model is known by most business leaders around the world. And still, in order to help the African-American community, you must give money to the ones who control them.

Politicians understand this. They call it "street money." President Obama refused to give money to pastors, and this is why many African-American pastors did not support him. Some would say that African-Americans did not support President Obama because of his stance on abortion and gay rights, but this is not the whole picture. Many who do not support Obama are the same ones who did support Hillary Clinton, who also supports abortion and gay rights. The real difference is that Hillary Clinton was willing to give the pastors money and pad their pockets. So their excuse against Obama is not truthful. The reality is that if a candidate does not pay the pastors, the pastors do not hold up that candidate to their congregation for endorsement.

Countless nonprofit organizations designed to support and build communities have attempted to enter the African-American community to build community centers and offer programs to help the people in them. The pastors have told these same organizations again and again that unless they give money to the pastors, they will be allowed no opportunity to help this community. Many projects that would help provide better institutions and programs in the African-American community will never gain a foothold in the door.

Why would a pastor discourage projects that are designed to help people and improve their lives? In my experience, these pastors like to control their congregations. They stand in the doorway to block these humanitarian projects from entering. These pastors would rather keep the control of their flocks all for themselves, even at the risk of ushering in fatherlessness, abortions, gangs, drugs and the many other ills that so infamously affect the African-American community—and other communities, too!

CHAPTER FOUR

The Marketplace and the Worship Center

The Marketplace

My studies show that the marketplace is where ministry happens. The Kingdom of God is to be revealed *outside* of the walls of a worship center. The marketplace is where believers spend most of their time, whether it is shopping, working, talking, listening or being with their family. Why would most of what Jesus shared in parables and teachings be marketplace-centered if He wasn't modeling something for us? I love Luke 10, where the disciples return saying the devils have been subject to them in Jesus' name. It demonstrates that being in the marketplace verifies the power of Jesus.

Where is the presence of light strongest? Obviously—it is in darkness. Why would the light hang around with light bragging about how bright it is? Even the dimmest light is able to blend in among the other lights. This is why so many believers are comfortable in their sin. They hang around in a room called a sanctuary and don't understand they are to *be* the sanctuary.

No matter how dimly your light shines, when you are in the presence of absolute darkness, your light reigns. This is critical to the Body of Christ. We currently have a huge identity issue and do not know who we are in Christ. When I visit the prisons and see the presence of God verified by those in absolute darkness, I become more encouraged to do the things of God. The darkness that consumes our country is more of an indictment of the Body of Christ than anything. The people who complain the loudest about their workplaces not having Godly leaders are believers. This tells me that the presence of these believers has not had any effect on the leadership of the company. Believers of today are not even carrying enough light to transform their marriages, families and workplaces. Yet, we make a living talking about how the president, Congress and other leaders are not making decisions from a Biblical worldview. Are you kidding me?

What do you expect from a person who does not know Christ and is totally left open to Satan? Not understanding the way in which the marketplace operates is a sign that the Body of Christ has no clue of its role. If you and I actually behaved in the marketplace as we pretend we do in the worship center, just maybe the world would want to know about Christ. If we treated our neighbors the way we pretend to treat the others in the pew, our neighbors might know the Lord. Whatever happened to 2 Chronicles 7:14 (NIV)?

If My people, which are called by My name, shall humble themselves, and pray, and seek My face, and turn from their wicked ways; then will I hear from heaven, and will forgive their sin, and will heal their land.

I guess that is just a good quote that doesn't mean anything to believers.

The marketplace respects hard work, discipline, team players, authority and productivity. This conflicts with the attitudes of the average Christian, since what we like is mediocrity, name it and claim it, giving our best to the worship center and pastor, and Christ being far away in Heaven. Romans 8:19 (KJV) says:

For the earnest of expectation of the creation eagerly waits for the revealing of the sons of God.

I witness this to be true, for I have hired many so-called Christians, yet I am still eagerly waiting for the sons of God to reveal themselves in the marketplace. The marketplace is begging for light in many ways to shine in its places of business.

The marketplace is where resources reside and are directed to accomplish whatever their lord desires. This is the place where the people, currency, gifts and knowledge, among many other things, reside and await a higher power for direction. How dare you sit in the worship center begging for resources to do the work of the Kingdom as if it has to come like manna from the sky? Do you not see how enormous the resources already are in the marketplace, and how much could be done for the work of the Kingdom if only you knew how to operate within it?

The telethons and fundraisers being advertised in the worship center and on Christian television are an absolute joke. I guess these rich pastors are hoping for their impoverished sheep to send them their lunch money, and maybe for some marketplace Kings to have pity on these little church folks. How dare those beggars say they are representing the Kingdom of God? The bankers, media advertisers, automotive dealers and many other marketplace leaders know, all too often, that the worst people with whom to do any business are Christian people. We see that Christians have all the theology in the world but no Kingdom authority.

The marketplace is where all decisions are made that affect the condition of the land. Many righteous marketplace leaders are wondering where to put their resources in order to secure the best return on investment. Yet, believers are struggling to give them any guidance because of their own stubborn refusal to submit to the things of God.

I am not telling you to conform to the world's way of doing things, but I am telling you to use your influence in the world. Believers are called to be beacons of light in the darkness, and the resources needed to accomplish the work of the last days are in the marketplace. Think of the impact that someone who is miraculously healed of God can have on a doctor, or a marriage restored on a business leader struggling in his own marriage. These two people, the medical doctor and business leader, may have great influence on other leaders. They may have gifts that God intends to use for His glory. But first, they need to witness the Lord working in the lives of believers with whom they come into regular contact.

Instead of being a testimony for the Lord's power, too many believers are caught up inviting people to their worship center. Jesus said to go to the people—to *reach out*, not to *drag in*.

I understand the biggest reason you may not be operating in the marketplace as a true Ambassador for Christ is your fear. Kings in the marketplace can smell fear and insecurity a mile away, and many believers are overcome with it. Yet the Christians who walk with their heads down and use passive words can be the very ones who play big shot in the worship center! Your deacons, pastors, bishops, trustees and other "churchy" positions are held by many people who act like little punks in the marketplace.

Can't you see that Christians are the only group of whom no one is afraid and whom no one wants to be like? The gangs will not threaten the Nation of Islam, but would kill the child of a Christian without even thinking twice. The same politicians who speak the name of God in vain off camera are those who condemn any hint of someone publicly talking about Mohammed. In a world where aggression is seen as strength and passiveness as weakness, your fear tells the marketplace that they have not found the Son of God in you.

I am not telling you to come out fighting as the world does, but I am saying your fear does not work in your favor in this situation. You cannot hide behind your big hat or psalms in the marketplace.

The marketplace is the place where all things happen, and the Church has turned it over to Satan. Both Christians and unbelievers are being defeated daily. Most prayer requests and spiritual warfare are coming from the marketplace because pastors refuse to send the sheep out amongst the wolves. If we tell the sheep Who their real King is, then maybe, just maybe, they will operate in His authority.

The Worship Center

God that made the world and all things therein, seeing that he is Lord of heaven and earth, dwelleth not in temples made with hands. (Acts 17:24, KJV)

The buildings that some Christians refer to as "the Church"—the place on which they spend so much money and in which they spend so much time—is of no importance to God. I know this statement makes those who brag about their buildings uncomfortable. So, let me explain.

I do not read that God is coming back for any building, outside of sitting in the temple in Jerusalem to declare Himself King of Kings and Lord of Lords.

God's word shows us that Jesus was preparing the disciples all along to minister in the marketplace. The revelation or information shared with the disciples was all part of the beginning of the process of their becoming transformed in their mind. Jesus told His disciples that the harvest is great, but the laborers are few. He is still saying the same today. Do we hear Him among all our conferences, building funds, fundraisers and in-fighting, which keep us too busy to harvest the Kingdom of God?

Yet, I have personally heard from the mouths of pastors that every time the church has a program, service or meeting, every member of the congregation should be present. That's right—closed up inside the worship center instead of doing the work of the Kingdom in the marketplace. Too many pastors are training the sheep to huddle in the barn and not graze in the field.

The most effective place into which to put our investments is in the work of the Kingdom. Giving to the building is not the same as giving to the Kingdom. Whenever a statement on the contrary is made in front of the Body of Christ, all true believers should cringe. The Kingdom of God does not operate in a worship center only, and this should never be implied again. The Kingdom of God is what we are to seek and abide in as Ambassadors in every area of our lives.

I have visited many pastors who want to show people around the building facilities as if these are somehow impressive. They are not! I am looking for shepherds who are ready to show off the sheep. Which is more important, the sheep or the barn that houses the sheep? I challenge all of you reading this book to tell anyone who is so excited about their building plans whether Christ is coming back for a facility or for His people.

As a marketplace leader of business, I am convinced, more than ever, that the smaller the overhead, the better the business model. If some pastors learned this lesson, perhaps they would not have huge debt and gigantic monthly overheads. Then they wouldn't need to lose sleep and dream up nightmare visions of all kinds of schemes and slicksters to milk the sheep. The pastors who have a building that is paid for can be just as bad, for they have simply finished the same process of wasting the resources on a building, while the sheep suffered and the community bankrupt.

I remember going to a worship center in Detroit, MI, that cost more than twenty-five million dollars while the entire twenty-block radius of the neighborhood was not worth twenty dollars. (I am joking, but you get the point.) The pastor was bragging to me about how they stayed within budget and completed the project on time. However, after six months of being in the new building, they were struggling to pay the light bill, not to mention the mortgage. I waited for cameras to come out with Ashton Kutcher saying, "You have been punked!" The cameras never came. The ones who were really being "punked" were the pastor and his congregation.

Who in their right mind would study anything about Jesus Christ and leave with a desire to build a twenty-five million dollar building in the midst of total destruction? The message this sends to the drug addicts, the poor, orphans and the hopeless in that community is that Jesus died so that we could build huge buildings while they and others die a slow death. This activity is laughable to marketplace leaders, who must provide a product or service and not an emotional guilt-trip to keep facilities open.

The worship centers in the Black community are, in many cases, worse since this community has usually never seen anything other than this errant model of worship centers that replace all real Kingdom work. It is obvious that the leadership in many of these organizations is not tracking the condition of the sheep but rather the dollars to the bottom line. If I were an overseer of this condition, I would be ashamed. But for far too many apostles, this has somehow become a badge of honor. Their seminaries are full of people ready to measure success by having a big building and a lot of people. This is a very demonic spirit, and it appears to be running wild in the Body of Christ.

You would not believe how many pastors are telling the people that their worship center is full of healing, salvation, deliverance and the presence of God—yet, no lives are being transformed. The sheep accept this unbelievable rhetoric without checking it, either literally believing it or not caring at all. Who told you that salvation, healing and God's presence are in a building? All of this activity should be happening in the homes, schools, street corners, companies, hospitals, prisons, mental facilities and anywhere there is darkness. The presence of God is *in His people*. If you say it is anywhere else, you are deceived. Read John 14:23 (NIV) and 1 Corinthians 3:9 (NIV) and tell me where Jesus said that He and the Father would reside in a building.

> *"Anyone who loves Me will obey My teaching. My Father will love them, and We will come to them and make Our home with them."* (John 14:23, NIV)

> *For we are laborers with God; ye are God's field, God's building.* (1 Corinthians 3:9, NIV)

If anything at all is occurring in the worship center, it occurs because the presence of God is in His people. If He can bring salvation to a person visiting a worship center, what could He do if millions of temples were sent into every neighborhood?

The Worship Center is Not for the Unbeliever

I will end this section with a statement that will probably challenge your current paradigms. Why would you invite unbelievers to a worship center? What do you expect unbelievers to do in a worship center, since they can't worship a God with whom they don't have a relationship by way of Jesus Christ? They do have a checkbook, and I guess that is all that matters when considering what the Church has become.

The few unbelievers who nevertheless give their lives to Christ inside a worship center are doing so because, when no ambassadors were sent out to them, they ran into the only place where they thought healing or restoration might occur. What does this tell us?

- The sheep are not being equipped during the worship service, since the pastor now has to spend that time preaching to the unbelievers in the audience. When you have unbelievers in the room together with believers, the worship, fellowship and equipping the believers is put on hold. Instead, the pastor is now being put in a position to preach.

- To preach the good news of Jesus Christ to someone who already has received Him as Lord seems a little strange to me. I don't read anywhere that preaching is for believers. I see in Ephesians 4 that the pastor and others of the five-fold ministry are a gift for the *equipping* of the saints. The worship meeting should be used to equip the believers in how to walk as God's new creation.

The only thing that should be shared during the worship session is who God is, who believers are in Him and how to go out and represent Him. I know this is totally foreign to many of us who only know tradition. However, this concept must be understood in order to allow the worship center to become a truly equipping place for the believers.

Instead, the worship center has been called a "church," which is not what it is. The believers *are* the Church.

CHAPTER FIVE

How Did We Get Here?

Our Troubled History

How did we reach the point where our Kings are not recognizing their true calling? This has troubled me. In my business conversations with other groups of people such as Jews, Anglos, Italians, Asians and Indians, I have found their conversation to sound more like the Kings of the Bible. Yet my conversations with African-American business-people usually make me want to run out of the room, just as I often do when I am around pastors.

Why do we have pastors primarily influencing our community? We must look at our history. The problems of the Black church are rooted in the horrors of slavery. As long as there were slaves in America, there were Christian preachers who cared to preach the Gospel among them and slaves who responded to God's word. In the days of slavery, the most nonthreatening individual in the Black community was a pastor. The pastor usually was the only one who knew how to read or how to communicate to the people "thus saith the Lord." The slave-master understood that if he left the pastor in the key role of leading the people, he could control the people through the pastor. Many history books refer to this method of control.

No slave-state permitted separate churches for the Black community. Perhaps, they were afraid of what would happen if Black people found out what the Bible really taught about slavery. Some churches provided special sections in their church buildings where Blacks could worship, out of the way of their White owners. Other denominations did not allow Black people to enter churches at all. They were literally not allowed to participate in any form of corporate worship.

In the northern states, there were a few Black churches, splinter-groups that based their theology and culture on the White denomination from which they had broken away. White overseers kept an eye over Black church conferences, sending a clear message that Black people could not be trusted to run their own churches. Even in the north, the idea that all Christians might worship together, regardless of skin-color or slave status, was simply unheard of in America.

By the time of the Emancipation, 11% of the Black population belonged to a church. Ninety percent were Baptists, and most of the rest were Methodists.

Throughout the next century, a distinctive Black Christian culture developed. This culture reflected, on the one hand, an enthusiasm for the Gospel, and on the other hand, the poverty, poor education and political oppression of the congregations.

Black Christians were enthused about the Gospel for all the same reasons that Christians throughout history have always been enthused about the Gospel. The Good News of a Savior-God who forgives sins, dwells among His people and promises eternal life brings hope to the most miserable and a challenge to the most complacent. Black worshippers in America have always been responsive and emotional—preaching is dramatic and has a charismatic flavor, and music has a strong rhythm. The negative side of this culture is that Black Christians expect to be entertained in church. In the 1930s, William Warren Sweet complained that Black churches contained more amusement than worship. If church services were boring, the Black worshiper would not return, and moral conduct outside of the worship center was often lax.

Black churches offer a simple, perhaps simplistic, theology that traditionally emphasizes repentance, salvation and grace. However, some Black preachers have departed from sound doctrine. Given low levels of education throughout the community, the average worshiper has been in no position to recognize the infiltration of heresy. Corrupt preachers have made themselves the center of personality cults. Father Divine referred to himself as "God incarnate," and Sweet Daddy Grace once said "grace could forgive people who sinned against God, but God could not forgive anyone who sinned against Grace."

The obvious social needs of the Black congregations have inspired a focus on social justice. This sounds fine. But when some pastors focused on social issues to the exclusion of preaching the Gospel, the fruit was bitter. The theologically-illiterate poor were attracted to teachers like Reverend Ike, who taught an early form of the "health and wealth" gospel. Those who heeded the call to worship money instead of Christ usually found that they did not become wealthy and were not automatically healed of every disease. And when their unrealistic expectations were disappointed, they were psychologically destroyed.

Churches became political stepping-stones for aspirant leaders. The civil rights movement was spearheaded by Black church leaders like Jesse Jackson, Adam Clayton Powell and Martin Luther King, Jr. Civil rights advocates usually maintained a *pretense* of Christianity, as no purely secular pathway to politics existed in the Black community. But not every civil rights advocate adhered to sound doctrine. Black churches were infiltrated by liberation theology, which was supposed to promise freedom to the oppressed Black community. This movement quickly abandoned Biblical theology, since it was primarily a political movement, and a violent one at that. At the extreme, Malcolm X abandoned Christianity altogether because Islam was better suited to his social goals—that is, less embarrassed by resorting to open violence and hatred.

In communities where only the pastors were educated, leadership was *only* possible via the Church. There was little call for Christian businessmen, lawyers, doctors, teachers and other "Kings" to change society. Not many Black people had the opportunity to enter these careers anyway. Ordinary poor Blacks had almost no political clout. Those who hoped to change the world placed the burden of changing it on the Black pastors. The pastor became all-powerful, the one person who had the social status and the knowledge to represent the needs of the Black community to the unfriendly White majority. People who were not pastors simply did not have an available avenue to do this.

Since the beginning of slavery, pastors have been put in position to control or influence Black people. I understand the need for that. During those horrific times, we needed to know "thus saith the Lord." We needed hope. We needed faith. Yet our social conditions today are far better, and still the old Church structure continues. We still expect the pastor to do the thinking for the whole congregation, while the congregation is expected to revere and obey the pastor. Further trouble arises when these same revered pastors are barely present in the congregation. Instead of declaring what the Lord saith, they are leaving their communities altogether. Have you not noticed when news and current affairs that primarily involve African-Americans appears on TV, they are represented by a pastor? What other group of people in the United States does this? None.

A hundred and fifty years after abolition, the culture of blind obedience is still entrenched in the minds of the docile Black congregation. The White "Masta" has been replaced by the Black "Pasta."

Killing With the Prosperity Doctrine

[1]*"Why should so few men be able to acquire all the gold?" Because they know how," replied the Chancellor. One may not condemn a man for succeeding because he knows how. Neither may one with justice take away from a man what he has fairly earned, to give to men of less ability."*

"But why," demanded the king, "should not all the people learn how to accumulate gold and therefore become themselves rich and prosperous?"

"Quite possible, your Excellency. But who can teach them? Certainly not the priests, because they know naught of money making."

"Who knows best in all our city how to become wealthy. Chancellor? Asked the king.

The question answers itself, your majesty. Who has amassed the greatest wealth in Babylon."

I have seen pastors manipulate God's people and cause them to fail in operating both in God's Kingdom and in man's. These pastors usually speak heavily on sin and prosperity. It does not make sense to preach

---

1 Clason, George S. 2002. *The Richest Man in Babylon.* New York, NY: Signet.

to God's people solely on prosperity and sin, for these topics are for the unsaved person. If pastors actually equipped God's sheep by teaching who God is and who the Christian is as a new man, and then sent the sheep out into the marketplace, and if the sheep then reflected this new man, who comes by way of Jesus Christ, then the marketplace would come to know Christ in a greater way.

A perverse message about money is frequently delivered to the Body of Christ. For example, Pastor Flashgold mostly preaches that "Money cometh." He brags about his kids having Mercedes-Benz and Lexus cars, sixteen-thousand-dollar dogs, jewelry and designer clothes. He runs on top of the money sat at his feet and tells the people it will now be blessed while the ushers come and pickup the funds to take to the back room. Whenever a pastor focuses on prosperity, he becomes the most prosperous person in the congregation. It is a matter of simple arithmetic. The pastor prospers when the people give him *their* money. But the prosperity principles are not transferable or duplicable to the people. Who is there to give money to the people who are usually already poor? No one. This is a direct example of a demonic spirit. When you see people walk up to throw money at the altar or hurl money at the pastor or stand in line to give money to the pastor's anniversary fund, soon comes destruction. The people are utterly deceived.

All Christians are supposed to think for themselves, and all Christians can compare what they hear in a worship service to what they read in the Bible! No true King would ever follow someone like Pastor Flash-gold, nor would he want to hire people who sit under such teachings.

Pastor Flashgold's glaring error is that he is teaching the importance of *money* and not of *principles*. I have heard many pastors say that your blessings are tied to the man of God, and if you support the man of God, you will prosper. This is only true to a small degree. It's good to support your local worship center. The truth is, your blessings are tied to the Man of God, Christ Himself. If you follow Him, you will indeed prosper *spiritually* and *physically*. Material prosperity, however, will be optional. Pastor Flashgold's flock has been terribly manipulated and controlled. When pastors teach such heresies, not only do they not enter into the Kingdom of Heaven, but they also stand and prevent others from entering. What perverse gate-keeping!

God's principles in financial matters are firmly tied into a process and a discipline, not to an emotion. Sound teaching on money and stewardship should concentrate on the disciplines of living, the excellence needed in the marketplace, the serving of one's community, the investment into others and doing the work of the Kingdom of God. Listen to what Paul says on this subject:

> *These are the things you are to teach and insist on. If anyone teaches otherwise and does not agree to the sound instruction of our Lord Jesus Christ and to godly teaching, they are*

conceited and understand nothing. They have an unhealthy interest in controversies and quarrels about words that result in envy, strife, malicious talk, evil suspicions and constant friction between people of corrupt mind, who have been robbed of the truth and who think that godliness is a means to financial gain.

But godliness with contentment is great gain. For we brought nothing into the world, and we can take nothing out of it. But if we have food and clothing, we will be content with that. Those who want to get rich fall into temptation and a trap and into many foolish and harmful desires that plunge people into ruin and destruction. For the love of money is a root of all kinds of evil. Some people, eager for money, have wandered from the faith and pierced themselves with many griefs. (1 Timothy 6:2-10, NIV)

The people who should be teaching on the principle of building financial wealth are those who have mastered wealth. Just like the books *The Richest Man in Babylon* or *Think and Grow Rich* teach on the fundamental principles of building wealth, so should the rich in the body of Christ. 1 Timothy 6 gives this instruction concerning the rich being teachers to the other members of the body in this area. When pastors are teaching on money to Blacks, they tell them to invest into their ministries as a way to wealth. This model keeps the pastor financially prosperous but not the people. Maybe this explains why Blacks have many times more worship centers per capita than any other group of people.

I was asked to teach a financial class in a worship center some years ago. The pastor and bishop, husband and wife, were White and most of the congregants were Black. The pastor and bishop are known for their extravagance as well as highly emotional approach, which is usually the recipe needed for White pastors to lead a congregation of Blacks. The class was for six weeks on early Sunday morning before the main service, and we started with ten people, which grew to one hundred and fifty within two weeks. The class attendees began to recruit others because of what they were learning. They were hungry to learn financial principles and how to apply them versus all they were taught from the pastor and bishop. You see, the people had never been taught on financial resources by someone who actually learned them through the marketplace. By the time we reached the final class, the attendees did not want to leave the room to go to the main sanctuary for their usual Sunday service. The bishop informed me in our final session that the people were learning so much that he felt threatened. It has been several years since I taught this class; however, I still get calls from attendees sharing how they have applied the principles in their lives and their financial situations have changed for the better. To God be the glory.

I challenge you to find other Christians who have success in applying fundamental financial disciplines to offer lessons for those seeking to gain wisdom in this area. Do not attempt to go into worship centers through pastors, but offer them in your training centers to the community of believers.

CHAPTER SIX

The King does not Want your Sheep

All who are under the yoke of slavery should consider their masters worthy of full respect, so that God's name and our teaching may not be slandered. Those who have believing masters should not show them disrespect just because they are fellow believers. Instead, they should serve them even better because their masters are dear to them as fellow believers and are devoted to the welfare of their slaves. (1 Timothy 6:1-3, NIV)

Slaves, obey your earthly masters with respect and fear, and with sincerity of heart, just as you would obey Christ. Obey them not only to win their favor when their eye is on you, but as slaves of Christ, doing the will of God from your heart. Serve wholeheartedly, as if you were serving the Lord, not people, because you know that the Lord will reward each one for whatever good they do, whether they are slave or free. (Ephesians 6:5-8, NIV)

I remember sitting in a meeting of marketplace leaders and hearing them say that the worst person to hire to work for you is a Christian. I was shocked to hear this statement, but I must say I have come to know it to be true. In more instances than I would have preferred, I have had to remove more Christians from being employees than any other group of people. I used to wonder why the Bible was not translating into their daily actions.

Actually, this question is not very difficult to answer. I grew up in a typical worship center that never addressed any of the work responsibilities of the Body of Christ. It blamed the devil or the White man for all its problems. I know, more than most, the issues racism has on the lives of people of all colors. But it pales in comparison to the damage that has been done from the pulpit.

That is why most business leaders would tell you the worst person to hire is a religious or Christian individual. Most so-called Christians do not operate in integrity, excellence, good service or with any other standard that reflects the Kingdom of God. Many Christians who worked in our businesses spent most of their work-time chattering on the phone to their friends, playing on the Internet, drinking coffee and demonstrating very little self-discipline. From where do they learn these behaviors?

I have observed African-Americans who come to job fairs wearing big baggy suits and loud-colored clothing. Where did they learn this custom? I have observed people who want to start their own businesses, yet they will not go and learn the business first. They say they were told all they had to do was just believe God and start up the company. Unsurprisingly, more than 90% of these businesses fail. Who told them that running a business does not require expertise? I have observed women who will cook their best meal for their pastor while their husbands and children eat tacos. Ah, there is the clue. I have observed people who will brag about their pastor and never mention the name of Jesus. Where does this behavior come from? It comes from their pastors.

Christians seem to have little understanding that their job is a ministry and that working with unbelievers is a great blessing from God. The workplace is one of the greatest places for ministry to occur, not by what someone says, but by the example of his life and by the results of his business. Christians should be the highest performers, best employees and most reliable people in the workplace. Yet this is not the case.

A King should desire to hire a Christian person more than one from any other group, since the teachings of Jesus Christ and principles of the Bible are desirable in the marketplace. Instead, Kings do not have in our businesses the very people we most need to help us operate our kingdoms in the ways of God. Such a poor job has been done preparing the Body of Christ for the workforce that the shoddy results are apparent in the marketplace. I mean this without any apologies.

Instruction for the sheep on how to operate in the marketplace is almost nonexistent in most congregations. The sheep produced by today's churches are very religious but not at all spiritual. They are lazy, have little to no integrity, feel entitled, are dramatic actors, self-pitying and sad. I did not expect African-American Christians to behave so badly, until I had hired enough of them to see a clear pattern. Perhaps you are offended by this statement. Well, so am I. I am an African-American who is a Christian, and I feel personally insulted to have witnessed so much evidence to support my accusation.

Christian employees talk very religiously, and that language is not effective in the marketplace. Their talking about what they are going to do far outweighs the action of what they actually do. Kings are looking for those who operate in excellence as unto the Lord and not cliché-talkers. Kings are looking for people who, like Daniel, are excellent in spirit. Daniel could be trusted to do the will of the King up to the point where it violated the laws of His God. Read the story of Daniel and it will be clear to you.

It pleased Darius to appoint 120 satraps to rule throughout the Kingdom, with three administrators over them, one of whom was Daniel. The satraps were made accountable to them so that the king might not suffer loss. Now Daniel

*so distinguished himself among the administra-
tors and the satraps by his exceptional qualities that the King planned to set him over the
whole Kingdom.* (Daniel 6:1–3, NIV)

Other reasons why Kings do not want to hire
these sheep includes lack of self-control and discipline,
they bring division, they lack integrity, and they are
unwilling to submit to authority.

The homes of most Christians are in terrible
shape, and Kings know that this dysfunction directly
affects performance. The total lack of balance in the
home comes from Christian leaders' lack of focus on
family and discipleship. The many issues that Christians bring to their workplaces as a direct result of their
lack of order at home are more than enough reason not
to hire them.

Too many Christians have no respect for time.
Any King will tell you that most Christians are known
for being late and having no regard for their own time
or other people's. This lack of discipline, in some cases,
comes directly from the pulpit, for they are showing
up late to worship services. If they can't be on time for
God's word, you know they can't be on time for work
either. I have personally invited pastors to business
meetings to connect them to businessmen who could
walk alongside them, and almost all of them have been
late. I wondered what kind of influence pastors are
having on people when they show no discipline in the
management of their time.

King Killer: A Lack of Self-Control and Discipline

I could write an entire book on this topic alone. One of the most obvious manifestations of a lack of self-control and discipline over one's life is being over-weight. Very few Kings want to hire overweight people for many reasons. These reasons include:

- Additional healthcare costs and missed work due to health issues;

- Lack of energy;

- Poor reflection on the company;

- Obvious lack of discipline;

- Poor attitude and outlook on life.

This obvious lack of discipline usually comes with the stereotype that many have of African-Americans. When you scan the crowd of an average African-American congregation, you see more overweight or obese people than most anywhere in the world. This must be addressed in order to position the sheep to be considered by marketplace leaders for employment.

I like to take my daughters to the gym because I want them to understand that working out is a part of a healthy lifestyle and that their daddy is not a lazy person, but is committed to being in shape. I want them to know and experience it. They don't come into the area where I am working out. They go into a designated kids center. I choose to expose them to a lifestyle that includes working out. We agree that most African-American women are overweight. I recently did a radio show on the topic, and I discovered that almost [1]70% of all African-American women are considered over-weight or obese. Experts have projected that 100% will be overweight in the next ten to twenty years. We must be willing to train our children and other members of the body how to live a healthy lifestyle. Unless a medical issue, this is a lack of self-control and attempt to cover other areas of pain.

No control over attitude and a poor outlook on life are more reasons that make hiring Christians an issue. A Christian should have a better outlook than anyone else, but this is unlikely to happen while churches teach that lack of self-discipline is acceptable, so people should just hold on until their life is over, and their blessing is coming one day when they get to heaven. This teaching encourages a terrible attitude. It means that Christians do not connect ministry with work. They show their best behavior on Sunday as if God is now watching and somehow did not see them acting the fool at work. We need deliverance from all our attitudes *soon*, before Christians self-destruct.

The fruit of the Spirit must become apparent in the lives of the believers or else they are not true believers in Christ. Jesus reminds us:

---

1 www.womenshealth.gov/minority-health

"I am the true vine, and My Father is the gardener. He cuts off every branch in Me that bears no fruit, while every branch that does bear fruit He prunes so that it will be even more fruitful. You are already clean because of the word I have spoken to you. Remain in Me, and I will remain in you. No branch can bear fruit by itself; it must remain in the vine. Neither can you bear fruit unless you remain in Me.

I am the vine; you are the branches. If a man remains in Me and I in him, he will bear much fruit; apart from Me you can do nothing. If anyone does not remain in Me, he is like a branch that is thrown away and withers; such branches are picked up, thrown into the fire and burned. If you remain in Me and My words remain in you, ask whatever you wish, and it will be given you. This is to My Father's glory, that you bear much fruit, showing yourselves to be My disciples." (John 15:1-8, NIV)

Kingdom Killer: Division

The Body of Christ is so segregated that most Christians do not even fellowship with people that don't look like them. Why would a King, who understands the importance of diversity, hire from a group of people who are known for their division? The Reverend Martin

Luther King, Jr., once said, "It is appalling that the most segregated hour of Christian America is eleven o'clock on Sunday morning. The marketplace recognizes more than ever the importance of cultural diversity due to the global connections in business, so why don't believers? I have observed the lack of interaction between Christians of different races, not only on Sunday, but on Monday through Friday in the marketplace. We may tolerate one another, but we don't see one another as true brothers or sisters in Christ. The sheep are divided by their loyalty to their shepherds and denominations. Whatever happened to Ephesians 4:6 NIV? "One God and Father of all, who is over all and living through all."

[2]According to the Center for the Study of Global Christianity (CSGC) at Gordon-Conwell Theological Seminary, there are more than 41,000 denominations of Christianity throughout the world. This division is absolutely ridiculous and does not deserve any further comment.

It is obvious there is no love between many fellow Christians, and it appears to be just what some shepherds desire. The body suffers a great deal because of our lack of unity, as well as our worship of the pastor and not the Master.

A real example of this issue came some years ago when I called together the five Black pastors of the largest congregations in my city to meet. The meeting was held at a local restaurant, since the pastors would

---

2 www.gordoncornwell.edu

not meet at any other worship center led by another pastor. In the meeting, I discussed the opportunity to work together for the good of the city to help bring together the body of Christ to focus on the needs of the community. I shared the details of the statistics concerning the land where all of their worship centers were in the city and how they compared to the other parts of the city. All the numbers were terrible, and I wanted to work with them to begin to address the condition of those living in the community. The response from all five pastors blew me away. They said, "We do not work together." I asked, "What do you mean?" Their response was simple, "We will not work together and do not like each other." I'm sure that in my ignorance, I was shocked to hear this response, since I thought it was about the sheep coming together.

Kings are concerned about the living of the people in the land, not the divide in the worship center. I challenge the marketplace leaders to begin to do things, as the Holy Spirit directs, to bring the body of Christ together in the land. We will need one another more than ever in the coming days. Seek out pastors who desire to see unity in the body of Christ, but do NOT let them hold you back.

Encourage unity. We have so much to offer one another and the glory of God will shine like never before.

King and Kingdom Killers: A Lack of Integrity

The lack of godly character is a huge marketplace issue from the viewpoints of leaders, employees and clients alike. The deceit undertaken by Christian employees is sometimes worse than that of unbelievers. It comes in the form of excuses for not turning up at work, stealing materials from the office, embezzlement, slacking on the job, looking for another job while being paid by the current employer, false résumé information and many other worldly actions. I understand the grace of the Father through Jesus Christ as well as the truth that all have sinned, but we should expect this type of behavior from those who are not equipped.

A Lack of Willingness to Submit to Authority

I will never forget an employee who was coming to work late more often than anyone else in the company. She told me that she worked for the Lord and did not answer to man. I told her, "The Lord said He has your paycheck waiting for you. So get it from Him."

This young lady was the typical religious person who had not been equipped to understand authority. While you are in your place of employment, the boss is your master. This is not to say that God is not your Lord, but authority can be delegated, and Jesus constantly refers to the owner of the business as your master.

Perhaps, it is significant that this lady spoke more of her reverence for her pastor than she did of Jesus. Most business leaders could share many examples of Christians bragging about their pastor and giving their best to the worship center, but do not witness of Christ or give their best to their workplace.

Similarly, Christians can show a complete lack of respect for our government officials. Now, I disagree with many government policies and with many officials' actions, just as you do. We live in a democracy, and we are entitled to disagree with whomever we like. This does not alter the fact that government officials are in a position of authority that was delegated to them *by God Himself*. We ought to respect that badge of office no matter what.

> *Let everyone be subject to the governing authorities, for there is no authority except that which God has established. The authorities that exist have been established by God. Consequently, whoever rebels against the authority is rebelling against what God has instituted, and those who do so will bring judgment on themselves. For rulers hold no terror for those who do right, but for those who do wrong. Do you want to be free from fear of the one in authority? Then do what is right and you will be commended. For the one in authority is God's servant for your good. But if you do wrong, be afraid, for rulers do not bear the sword for no reason. They are God's servants, agents of wrath to*

bring punishment on the wrongdoer. Therefore, it is necessary to submit to the authorities, not only because of possible punishment but also as a matter of conscience.

This is also why you pay taxes, for the authorities are God's servants, who give their full time to governing. Give to everyone what you owe them: If you owe taxes, pay taxes; if revenue, then revenue; if respect, then respect; if honor, then honor. (Romans 13:1-7, NIV)

I urge, then, first of all, that petitions, prayers, intercession and thanksgiving be made for all people— for kings and all those in authority, that we may live peaceful and quiet lives in all godliness and holiness. This is good, and pleases God our Savior. (1 Timothy 2:1-3, NIV)

A Lack of Excellence in Spirit

The standard by which Christians do things should be higher than other people's standards, for we are working unto the Lord. Why is this so rarely the case in today's church? Most of us are receiving teaching that does not include much of a standard of excellence. I can't tell you how many times I have wondered who it is that is supposed to be teaching the sheep how to operate in their daily lives. This question so often sits on my mind when I see the sheep out in public and observe that they are acting like wild animals.

I was told by my business mentor never to hire someone with a dirty car, as this person will have a dirty office and cost us money: lost files, disorganization and a spirit of dysfunction. He was right! I noticed that the very people with a Jesus sticker on the car were those who kept their cars on the inside like hillbillies. The standard by which Christians do things should be an example to the world, yet the only thing that appears to be the priority is to get through the doors of the worship center.

I know too many people who say they are Christians, yet they have more problems in their lives than unbelievers. Their family and financial structures are all out of order. There is no discipline in their lifestyle. This spills over, not only in them being chronically late, but also in unproductive work. It is impossible to be productive when their whole lifestyle is in bondage to one idol or another. The difference in their output will be obvious to everyone. Even an unbeliever who gets drunk the night before will still show up at work and do his job. Everybody understands that. Yet a Christian who is having issues at home will bring personal problems into the workplace, and productivity just plummets. Everyone notices how they are exuding that spirit of confusion.

The reason why I don't want your sheep is that your sheep carry the very spirits that I expect from the world. A leader likes to have a culture of discipline. Leaders not only like to operate with discipline, but they create an environment that welcomes discipline.

Most believers, if we can be honest, do not operate with discipline. This is a sign that they have not been taught correctly, for *discipline* is the root word of *discipleship*.

Religious sheep are extremely hypocritical. They will in one voice talk about the things of God, and in that same sentence not understand that they are subject to the boss' authority. They will not do what the boss instructs them to do. How can a person be subject to the God of the Bible and then not understand the authority that a King has been given? The Lord takes it further and says:

> *Servants, be obedient to them that are your masters according to the flesh, with fear and trembling, in singleness of your heart, as unto Christ.* (Ephesians 6:5, KJV)

If the sheep truly grasped this, then they would work for the King as if they were serving the King of Kings. They would not serve the earthly King in recognition of that King's personal qualities. He might be a drunk and cursing King. They would serve him as if they were serving God out of respect for his position of authority. They would serve in integrity, in spite of the King's issues. The King might well know that he personally does not deserve such service—his position of authority is what demanded it. The King would receive the benefit of the sheep's obedience to God, and so he would promote them. He would look at that Joseph or Daniel and realize he must put that person at his right hand.

Even when the King's god is different from his employee's God, he will still promote that worthy employee. He will let himself be influenced by his employee and come to know his God. Daniel was able to say, "God has found no fault in me, and I have done you, the King, no wrong." (Daniel 6:21-22, KJV) God, his ultimate authority, found no wrong in Daniel. He had done no wrong to King Darius' position of authority.

But none of this will happen if the employee does not respect the King's authority. The King will never put at his right hand an undisciplined, religious person who ignores his instructions.

Christians have the opportunity to collect their business associates for the Lord as harvest. Yet these very people say that they don't even want to be around Christians. I have seen it happen many times. When someone gives you a business card with that little fish sign, the *Ichthus*, that represents that he or she is a Christian, what impression does that create? When a King who is not a Christian sees that on a business card, he will most often throw it in the trash. He has come to know that Christianity means no standard.

Unhappy Christians often blame the King for their condition. They accuse him of removing them, firing them or not promoting them. Then the priest prays and shouts over them. It does not occur to the priest to go to the King and ask why he removed that sheep. Such feedback would help the priest prepare the sheep to do better for the next job. The priest doesn't have the right to question why a King removed somebody, but he can, on behalf of the sheep, follow up with the King. Similar to an exit interview, the priest can inquire as to why the sheep needed to be removed.

Why would a priest want to ask such a sensible question? That would be like saying, "The very sheep that I was equipping to be in your place of business, who you should have recognized as your best employee and promoted, has instead been fired. So we must have taught that sheep wrongly." What priest wants to hear bad news about his own mistakes? What priest has the courage to return to God's word and teach the sheep something useful to apply to his next job? This is not happening.

The priest can absolutely be the catalyst by which restoration happens in the marketplace. But it will only happen if the priest walks with a King and sits down with him to ask that question. Priests prefer to say, "The Devil is a liar!" They do not want to hear that the sheep who put on their best faces for the two hours they are at worship center, go into the King's kingdom to play the fools.

A Lack of Financial Insight

I can hardly think of one Christian who has worked for me who did not beg for money outside of his contracted pay. Christians are constantly coming to ask the King to loan them money, and they do not seem to have any consciousness that this presumptuous request is way outside of their role. Their role is to serve in the kingdom by doing their job in exchange for which they receive wages. The wage was agreed at the time both signed the contract. Yet many of them have come to ask for a loan or a raise. I do not mean they wanted advances on their paychecks. Although this also would have been outside the terms of the contract. They wanted money for which *they had not worked.*

Sometimes Christians fall into genuine hardship. When that happens, they should be able to go to the storehouse. It is up to the church community to provide for brothers in need. But they cannot beg aid from the storehouse because there is nothing there— the wealth of the church has all been swallowed up by buildings. [3]A recent study by the Barna group says 99.7% of church spending goes towards payroll and building expenses. Other times, when Christians beg their employers for money, they are not in need. It is simply greed.

Who influenced Christians to be greedy? Who taught them they could ask for whatever they liked and expect to receive it automatically? Sheep are influenced by their shepherd. If the shepherd and elders are not teaching true principles of how to operate and how to acquire sufficiency, the sheep will not learn how it should be done. What they are seeing from their shepherd is "money cometh" by way of your asking for it. So

3 www.barna.org

they copy. They come to the King and ask for resources that they have not earned. The only resource that they have the right to ask from the King is that for which they have worked. Believers have a spirit of entitlement, and in most cases, it is ingrained in them from the pulpit. Another way you can tell this is true is by the desire to establish a non-profit. I hear them say, I have a non-profit that I need you to support or help me get a grant. This mindset is definitely not from a King's influence.

If they came to the King to say they need money and asked what they could do to earn it, then the King would possibly see how he could increase their hours. Or he might investigate if they merited an increase in their responsibilities and hence in their rate of pay. That way, more money could be fairly earned. A King might even probe to ask them what they are currently doing that is causing them to be in this shape. Is it really due to insufficient incomings, or is it about inappropriate outgoings? People who truly want to solve their problems in a godly way would be glad of this kind of help.

Unfortunately, what I have found is when I did give out a loan, it never came back on time—if it came back at all. If I asked about the money, the borrowers were affronted and became mad or offended. Sometimes they even quit, knowing they had a debt to repay. When I have probed them about how they ended up in financial difficulties, the question also made them angry. These people never figured out that I was probing them in order to discover the hole through which their money was seeping. You can only patch a hole if you know where it is!

The best thing I can give such people is information. But they don't want my information for it contradicts what they hear in church, where they learn that the highest form of development is not from application or direction but from entertainment. Then they try to apply that principle in the marketplace. When it doesn't work, they become angry. All they need to do is ask the King to teach them what they need to know. So they go to every job with that same demanding spirit, and every job fails in the same way.

I have explained countless times that "Money cometh" is a lie. Money does not come by way of your demanding it. When you ask for money, you demonstrate that, at the very foundation, you do not understand it. A pastor is never supposed to ask for money. The people desperately need to be taught what the Master desires from them. If you believe that the Master desires tithes and offerings, then teach the people how to hear the Master's voice, so He can tell them what He wants them to give. Too few pastors are teaching that way about money. Instead, they are using their voices, coercion, manipulation, tactics, two-hundred-and-fifty-dollar handkerchiefs and one-thousand-dollar offering lines to collect it.

Then the sheep try to take that attitude into the marketplace. The very foundation of the attitude is wrong, and I don't want sheep who think like that. He does not belong to the Great Shepherd; he belongs to his local pastor. When the sheep mimics the pastor, I know the pastor owns that sheep. Sheep that mimic their pastor do not truly represent the Kingdom of God.

A King may be an unbeliever and not know the Kingdom of God. In that case, the sheep are supposed to be modeling Kingdom ways so that King will one day come to them and say that he has noticed the way they operate with their spouse, finances, health, or whatever it may be. That unbelieving King is watching how the Kingdom of God is manifesting in that believer. If it appears to be something that the King desires, the very person to whom he will go is the sheep sitting right there in his office. He can sit the sheep down and say that he has this issue and ask for some advice. A true King has no problem asking for advice from a citizen of his kingdom if that citizen represents a better way. Conversely, if that citizen is operating in a worse way, the King won't want to keep that sheep as his citizen. He is looking out for the people whose results are different. Unfortunately, when he peruses the crowd of his employees, the average Christian does not shine.

I see people in darkness looking for light. When a King is seeking light, he walks to the window. He literally looks out of the office window for someone who is shining. If an employee shines, he calls him or her in, just as God did to Isaiah. In most cases, however, that shining employee is not a sheep from the Christian flock.

CHAPTER SEVEN

Where Are the True Kings?

Kings are all around us. Kings are sitting right in our neighborhoods, corporate offices, schools, prisons and gangs. But we don't know how to identify them. Those who can really lead (influence) and are anointed to develop your community are sometimes found in gangs, especially in the African-American community. The gang leader understands authority and dominion and—as misguided as he may be—demands complete obedience. As a matter of fact, if you don't do what he is telling you to do by his bylaws, then he will either beat you down or he will kill you. A kingly mind expects total obedience to the laws that he puts forth, and most of us don't understand this.

I recently gave a speech at a local prison, and I asked the room of about twenty-five young men, "How many of you would call yourself a leader?" All of them raised their hands. I then asked them if they even knew what a leader was, and their response was, "Yes!" I asked them to elaborate, and they were clear in their understanding of leadership. I then asked them how they led. They told me how they led their gangs, how they established businesses through drugs and prostitution, and how they controlled their neighborhoods. I became quite interested in hearing more, since I had hardly ever heard from people who understand leadership. Interestingly enough, these leaders were sitting behind prison bars.

I asked them, "If you are leaders, how is it that you are in prison?"

Their answer was, "That's all we know."

I can relate to that since, as a youth, I used to do a lot of things that were not godly. I also grew up in a neighborhood where people would not talk legitimate business, but youths were taught how to sell dope, hustle and scam people. In the African-American community, most of us have never been asked for our business ideas or for our vision because we are not influenced by business leaders, but we are influenced by pastors.

If you try to force a King to conform to a system that is not what he is built for, he will drop out. He will quit if someone is trying to force him to be something that he is not. The system is trying to turn him into a follower, and this system is killing the ones who have the ability to turn our communities around. They can turn things around because that is what they are called to do. I see them when I go into the detention centers. When I speak to them, there is the same gift. For when a King is speaking to Kings, they respond. They respond in a way of brokenness, knowing that they are in the room with someone who has the same gift that they themselves carry—yet no one has recognized it.

Instead, we are trying to preach at them. No! We must *speak* into them. There are leadership gifts within these misfits. All over this country, pastors are allowing true Kings to die whenever they fail to support misguided Kings. Their community is only conditioned to support priests and to build multi-million-dollar domes. In this way, they have created dead communities. [1]Priests, over the last thirty years, have spent five hundred and forty billion dollars on worship centers. *540 billion dollars*—and you have nothing to show for it. You have created nothing that will make your community thrive. Yet pastors have the nerve to look at me as if I'm crazy. I am telling you that you must change this model. It is not of God; it is demonic; it is manipulative; and it is the absolute spirit of the enemy.

In the African-American community, the businessmen are usually the guys who run drugs, run the numbers, are pimps or are loan sharks. I am convinced that the African-American community is built to kill

1 www.generouschurch.com/churches-spend-money-internally

Kings. We are taught to support the pastors but not to support the business of the kings. Many of these lessons came from slave masters who used slavery for economic gain. Many Whites felt threatened when Blacks considered spending their money amongst themselves. History verifies the assault on anyone of color who tried to establish economic independence for their families and community.

We are told to give tithes and offerings to the Church and that will somehow bring us through financially; then we will acquire more stuff and we will be in position for wealth. This is not what the Word of God says. The Word of God says:

> *"Bring the whole tithe into the storehouse, that there may be food in My house. Test Me in this," says the Lord Almighty, "and see if I will not throw open the floodgates of heaven and pour out so much blessing that there will not be room enough to store it."* (Malachi 3:10, NIV)

Please explain to me how you translate "storehouse" into "worship center?" Last time I checked, a storehouse contains material for future use. Suppose you need to get back on your feet financially. Or suppose you've had a great idea that needs funding. I suggest you go to your worship center, where you have been tithing, and see if there is anything in the storehouse. You already know what will happen.

With all that has been taught concerning giving, why are our communities in the worse shape since slavery? The fundamental teaching in the African-American community is tied to a model that will never allow it to prosper but will predominately cause it to fail. The results speak for themselves. Those young men in prison showed me that the ones whom God intended to lead the community are sitting in prison, fighting in gangs or lying in early graves.

The day after I left the prison, I had to give a speech to a group of twenty-five high school students. This was the same number that was in the prison the day before. I asked the same question of these teenagers, "How many of you would call yourself leaders?" Only one young lady raised her hand. After elaborating on what leadership was, I later asked the question again. Still no more than two or three raised their hands. While on my way home that afternoon, God spoke to me and said, "Your Kings are in jails, and your followers are being forced to lead." This made it clear to me that my community is killing the Kings.

The primary culprits who are allowing this to happen are the pastors. You may be thinking, "Joel, that's a tough statement." I know. I wish it were not true.

The more I travel to detention centers, prisons and street corners of idle young men, not exclusive to race, the more convinced I become that many of these young men are called to lead. Consider the organizations and resources these young men build with their illegal activity. What would these same youths be able to do if they were taught business skills and lived in communities where not surviving but thriving was the priority of the day? If you consider the fact that most leaders have been through tough life circumstances, have dropped out of school, and have had to fight for themselves since birth, these young men are exactly the same as some of the most successful businessmen in Corporate America.

No one even considers asking these young men about their ideas, creativity or anything else, since we don't consider them to be contributors to society. Sadly, our court system is totally designed to catalyze their destruction, as it is more popular to lock them behind bars than to give them direction and an environment where they can thrive.

Consider people like Sean Combs (Puff Daddy), 50 Cent, Jay-Z and others who came from these communities and used entertainment to escape. Michael Jordan, Magic Johnson, Bill Cosby, Dr. Cornell West and many others used other ways to escape from the priest-controlled neighborhoods, and they now contribute greatly to society. All of these guys are more businessmen than entertainers or athletes, but they come from a community that will only support churches, entertainers and drug dealers. How else could they have demonstrated their great business talents unless they used the only pathways that Blacks will support?

Look at Bill Gates, Michael Dell, Mark Zuckerberg, Dustin Moskovitz, Eduardo Saverin and Chris Hughes of Facebook, Larry Page and Sergey Brin of Google, and you will see that many of them dropped out of school to pursue their business endeavors and build their kingdoms. The more likely someone is to be a King, the less likely he is to remain in traditional education systems. [2]That is why we have a national average of more than 50% of African-American boys dropping out before graduating from high school. While not all of these boys are Kings-in-the-making, their dropping out has to do with family, environment and not receiving any real instruction. There is no true system built in which they can thrive, so they end up leaving school and going to the streets. The streets are a broken community that will never support their vision of building businesses. The streets can only support them by drug-dealing, pimping and similar street folly. This happens whenever priests control their communities.

Do you honestly believe the only guys with this kind of talent are the famous ones mentioned above? NO! Many more are sitting idle and wasting away because we don't let Kings run the community. These same young men have taken control over many of our communities by using drugs, gangs and so on. It is their nature to lead and govern, but without the right leadership in the community, they will lead in the wrong ways.

The only young men in our community who usually receive support are athletes, as they are celebrities to some people. Think about how fundamentally ignorant it is to glorify someone for his sports skills while we spend little to no time developing his life

---

2 www.blackboysreport.org

skills. Why do you think Michael Vick, Allen Iverson, Terrell Owens, Dennis Rodman and others self-destruct once they win big contracts? Notice how many pastors in the local community position themselves to receive some of the proceeds from these athletes. Look at how many of these pastors are starting schools that focus on athletics. It is for the money. You will find few to no entrepreneurial schools in our community, given that the people in leadership are pastors who care more about worship centers, being in control and having money in their pockets than about the true growth of the community.

I was a product of a priest-led community, and it led me down a path of mischief. I can only imagine the levels of success and prosperity that our community would generate if we truly allowed the Kings to lead. The same skills that now cause disaster and fear would be used to bring prosperity and hope. The Saul of the world became Paul of the Kingdom of God. What about the transformation that could happen with these young men and women if the pastors actually fed the sheep and sent them out to do the work in the marketplace?

We have to grab our young men. We have to seize them from the prisons and street corners. We must speak into them what they really are and support them. We must put them in environments where they are going to be around other Kings, who will help speak into them and develop them. If we don't do this, then they will continue to die, just like the communities that created them. The African-American community is in bad shape and is dying.

How does a King Know he is a King?

There are two ways in which a King knows he is a King. One way is when a mature King can identify him. The other way is when a priest, hearing who the Kings are from the Father, can identify them. When I go into the prisons, I am able to speak to the youths differently because a King is speaking to Kings.

When the average priest enters a prison, he doesn't tell them they are Kings. He preaches at them. We have to tell these priests to step aside and let the Kings rise up. If that priest does not want to go back and shepherd the sheep in his flock, he may well refuse to step aside when the Kings rise up. Now the priest is fighting for dominance. He can't win that war, although, he can successfully manipulate and control the weak and sabotage the calling of the Kings. In other words, the priest can ensure that everyone loses equally.

In the same way, while Jesus was in their midst, the Pharisees and scribes still won some people. Some people followed them out of a liking for the tradition and the comforting idea of someone else controlling and manipulating them. People who don't know who they are don't want to be sent out. They want to be controlled. They want to sit up all day under somebody who offers a place of comfort, like a child who never wants to leave his mommy. When the father, a real man, is around, he will kick them out and tell them they have to go. We can expect a fight from those African-American priests who have acquired wealth from leading the community and have enjoyed being in control. They will not relinquish that control without a protest.

Finding & Guiding the Misplaced Kings

When you create a community that believes in building facilities more than people, a community that has made the people believe the only place God wants them to support is the worship center, the true Kings will be destroyed or misplaced. The testimonies of the business people who have gone into these prisons to teach business and come out blown away by the talents of the inmates provide validity to the concept of a misplaced King. Those who are truly called to lead will lead no matter what. But without appropriate mentoring, they will lead the wrong ventures in the wrong ways.

These misplaced leaders are still undergoing challenges. They are battling and fighting to survive. A leader is being attacked consistently in every small town, and mid-size and large market throughout our country. The one who has been called to lead is very often an African-American boy. I'm not excluding others who are out there, but I'm talking about these boys in particular, as they are under such attack and have very poor leadership in the community. This is the group that is being locked up the most. Let's take a closer look at this.

Under today's leadership, [3]more than 900,000 African-American men currently sit in prison. In contrast, only 45,000 African-American males graduated college this year. Look at the staggering difference—45,000 college graduates versus 900,000 prisoners. For every one African-American who graduates, twenty go to prison. There are two things that you must recognize. One is that the enemy understands this and wants to deceive us into thinking that his attacks are not tied to race. The enemy despises all people, and his goal is to destroy all human communities. He wants to destroy a young man of color because he knows that the Black community is wrongly set up and misaligned. It's easy prey, a community that is already all but conquered. The enemy knows that if young Black men continue to do what they are doing, they will destroy their own community. It is not hard to figure this out. Look at the numbers. Every Black youth who we leave to the enemy is another strike against our whole community.

I recommend going into local prisons, detention centers, drop-out programs, gang locations and anywhere where you can find the misplaced Kings, and investing some of your resources into them. If a person has less than one year left on his prison sentence, go and teach him business skills, then fund his idea once he is

---

3 www.naacp.org

released. One year gives you plenty of time to test his commitment and willingness to operate a business and lead his community. You can use the Internet to facilitate many of these classes, and I'm sure with all the budget cuts from the state and federal governments, you would be welcomed with open arms. The instructors or facilitators should be people with a proven track record of success in business or should be retired military officers. I have found that the inmates show greater respect to men than to women, so I recommend having women with the gift of administration work behind the scenes, while men teach the sessions.

Another way to reach these much-needed marketplace leaders is to stop running the same old radio and television programs. Instead, use these media to influence people to build programming to equip the misguided Kings. Both priests and Kings normally have advertising budgets and contacts that can minimize the cost. Just think of the image your company or worship center would portray from doing these good works.

Go into the schools and ask about students who seem to be on the road to destruction. They show signs of greatness, but they need direction and more guidance than basic schools can offer. I promise you there are many misplaced Kings out there, and it is our responsibility to seek them out.

Imagine what our communities would look like if we actually did what the Bible teaches. Do you ever wonder why the Word tells us to go to the lost, like in prisons and other places where most Christians have been told not to go? I am totally convinced if we, as

Americans, especially Black Americans, don't begin to connect to and direct our youth to new forms of teaching and empowerment, we are going to become the land of the has-beens.

Go and Get your Kings to Establish their Kingdoms

The need for marketplace Kings is absolutely enormous, but it requires the many pastors who have controlled the communities to move aside. I have stated in previous chapters how significant it is for us to create a culture where leadership is supported and visions and dreams are welcomed.

There are specific steps that must be taken in order to establish kingdoms upon the earth. Here is what must be done:

1. **Identify the Kings.** This process takes both Kings and priests. While it takes a King to speak into the life of another King, a priest is necessary to provide guidance in identifying whom the Lord has selected as His Kings. This eliminates confusion as to who is ordained to walk in the position of a King and whom the Lord considers to be a shepherd of His people. The priest will hear what saith the Lord and confirm those who are called as Kings.

2. **Replace pastors in community leadership positions with Kings.** In order to have proper balance in both the Kingdom of God and the kingdom of marketplace, Kings must take their rightful places at the helm of leadership. Kings must communicate their authority to lead in the community, so the pastors can return their attention to shepherding and equipping their flock in the ways of the Lord. Both Kings and priests must stay in the lanes the Lord gave them, so this transition can happen as peacefully and smoothly as possible.

3. **Establish programs and schools that teach marketplace principles.** Marketplace principles of business must be taught to both Kings and priests in order for a kingdom to operate effectively and efficiently. Only a true King can speak to the inner operations of a business and achieving success in the marketplace. Because of this natural role, it is the Kings who must create the model to lead the schools and raise up other Kings, just as there are currently programs that teach and raise up priests led by other priests or those with the gifts of the five-fold ministry.

These schools should include mentoring and assessment of the up-and-coming Kings' maturity and readiness to enter the marketplace. I recommend challenging the current marketplace Kings to establish these schools as both classrooms and workplaces in their communities. Kings and priests must work together to provide the assessment tools to promote and properly ensure these future Kings' success— spiritually, financially, emotionally, intellectually and physically.

Could such a venture succeed in the African-American community? Of course it can. Our community is full of "losers" who defied all the naysayers and became unqualified winners.

Chris Gardner Pursues Happiness

Chris Gardner[4] is an entrepreneur, stockbroker, writer and philanthropist. He funded part of a $50 million project that created low-income housing and employment opportunities in San Francisco. He helps with careers counseling, job placements and comprehensive job training for the homeless population and at-risk communities in Chicago. He serves on the boards of the National Fatherhood Initiative (NFI) and the National Education Foundation, sponsors shelter programs for the homeless and two annual education awards. In 2002, he received the Father of the Year award from the NFI. His autobiography, *The Pursuit of Happyness*, was published in 2006.

The man who drove this quintessential success story had the most miserable childhood imagin-

4   en.wikipedia.org/wiki/chris_Gardner

able. His biological father abandoned him before he was born, and his stepfather was so violent that the children feared for their lives. His mother was put in prison twice—once on false charges and a second time for trying to kill her husband—leaving Chris and his sisters to the mercies of foster care. While in care, Chris bonded with his uncle Henry, but Henry was drowned in the Mississippi the following year.

Gardner decided early on to work hard and become wealthy. He toyed with medicine and sales before a chance encounter with a stockbroker in a red Ferrari inspired him to become a stockbroker. After multiple interviews, he was accepted into a training course, so he quit his steady job—only to find that his assigned training manager had been fired, and he was no longer enrolled in a stockbroking course. At this point, his girlfriend dumped him, and he was sentenced to ten days in jail for unpaid parking tickets, which he accumulated while job hunting. After this dramatic setback and with a CV of no education, no work experience, no savings, no connections and a jail term, Gardner did manage to secure a trainee position. He worked very long hours and made two hundred calls a day to prospective clients. He passed his licensing exam on the first attempt and became a full employee of the firm.

Unfortunately, his salary was not enough to meet living expenses. It was at this point that his ex-girlfriend left their child with him, making him a single father in an apartment that did not allow children. Gardner and his son became homeless. For nearly a year, they ate in soup kitchens, and slept in his office, on park benches, or in railway stations, while the baby spent his days in daycare. Gardner never mentioned his problems to his colleagues. His son recalls, "I couldn't tell you that we were homeless. I just knew that we were always having to go. So, if anything, I remember us just moving, always moving."

Eventually, the Methodist Church allowed them to stay at a shelter for homeless women. Gardner was able to establish his own brokerage firm, Gardner Rich & Co, in Chicago in 1987. He began by working from home, with only $10,000 starting capital and his work desk, which doubled as his dinner table. Twenty years later, after committing long hours to solid business practices, he was a multi-millionaire.

How did Chris Gardner overcome his circumstances? He attributes his success to a "never give up" attitude, fuelled by the example of his mother and the expectations of his children. His mother never made her personal problems an excuse for self-pity. She told her children, "You can only depend on yourself. The cavalry ain't coming." How many other youngsters in "hopeless" situations could learn to depend on themselves and make constructive choices, if only an adult like Bettye Jean Gardner inspired them? How many more would succeed if only they had easier access to homeless shelters, careers counseling or on-the-job training?

Jay-Z Pursues Music

The famous rapper and song-writer Jay-Z (Shawn Corey Carter) has sold fifty-million albums, has received fourteen Grammy awards, owns the sports bar 40/40 Club, is the creator of the urban clothing brand Rocawear, and is worth nearly half a billion dollars. He uses his influence to raise awareness of the global water shortage, to urge citizens to use their vote, and to donate to disaster relief.

Yet Jay-Z's childhood sounds like a social worker's notes on how to set up a client on a straight path to jail. He was born in a New York housing commission that he describes as "a dangerous place to live," riddled with gangs, drug-dealing and high crime rates. His father abandoned the family. When he was twelve, he shot his brother in the shoulder. During high school, he sold crack cocaine and did not graduate.

How did he become an entrepreneur? His mother recognized him as a drummer when his siblings complained that he had kept them awake at night by banging drum patterns on the kitchen table. She bought him a boom box for his birthday. Then he was mentored by Jonathan Burks (Jaz-O). When no major label would give them a record deal, Jay-Z and two friends created Roc-A-Fella Records as their own independent label and struck a deal with a distributor. His album *Reasonable Doubt* reached number 23 on the Billboard 200 and eventually hit platinum status. His next album, *My Lifetime I*, was recorded at a low point when he was grieving the death of a friend. It sold better than *Reasonable Doubt*.

Once again, the morals of the story are work hard, don't give up, try new ways of doing things, and have a mentor. A mentor can provide the acceptance and approval that young people so desperately need, together with guidance towards a suitable career choice. Young people become "lazy" when they assume that nothing they do will ever produce any results. When their efforts are rewarded, they are likely to repeat them.

Psychologists have been telling us for a hundred years that people repeat actions that bring rewards, but they stop behaviors that lack consequences. If a young person is bored at school, is never commended for finishing homework, and doesn't see how these "studies" will lead to a job later, he is very likely to stop going to school. If his classmates "reward" him by laughing at the way he bullies the teacher and paying him cash for drugs, he might continue attending school, but only so that he can clown around in class and sell drugs in the schoolyard. The truth is that it's just as rewarding to make people laugh on a floodlit stage as it is in the classroom; it's just as rewarding to sell cars or clothes as it is to sell drugs. Where a mentor can help is by showing the young person how the same talent, used constructively, can bring him the same reward as when it was used destructively.

Dr. Haller's Leaders

Dr. Howard Edward Haller's doctoral research was a series of interviews with leaders who had overcome serious adversity. Some of his participants suffered ordinary challenges, others endured the most extraordinary adversity. Here are some of his success stories.

- **Schaja Shachnowski** was a Jewish Holocaust survivor who became Major General in the U.S. Army.

- **Monzer Hourani** watched his mother being murdered in the Lebanese Civil War before becoming a real estate entrepreneur in Texas. His firm, Medistar, survived the real estate crisis of the 1980s.

- Dr. **Tony Bonanzino** grew up in a horrific "care" home for fatherless boys. He lived to buy out his employer and become the C.E.O. of the pharmaceutical business, Hollister-Steir Labs.

- Dr. **Blenda Wilson** suffered discrimination for her race, her gender and her age, but she was a leader in education policy and reform. She became a University Chancellor and University President.

- **Daniel Inouye** grew up in poverty and lost his arm in World War II. He became an attorney and long-time U.S. Senator (D-Hawaii).

- **Orrin Hatch**'s family was impoverished during the Great Depression, and he lost a brother to war; he had to work his way through high school, college and law school. He has been a U.S. Senator (R-Utah) for thirty years.

- **H. H. "Zig" Ziglar** was born into a large, poor rural family. His father died when he was five. He initially failed in sales until he found himself an effective mentor. He went on to build a nationwide training and motivational speaking firm.

- Dr. **John C. Malone** worked his way through high school, college and graduate school; fought business and regulatory battles; suffered the death of his mentor and majority shareholder; but turned a small, struggling cable firm into a $58 billion company. He is currently Chairman and C.E.O. of Liberty Media Inc.

- Dr. **Nido R. Qubein** arrived in America with $50, and he spoke not a word of English. He nevertheless went to High Point University, built several major marketing firms and has ownership in a leading financial institution. He is now a University President and is a major leader in the National Speakers Association.

- Dr. **John Sperling** was born in poverty, was dyslexic and semi-literate, but he acquired a Ph.D. from Cambridge. He became the founding Chairman and C.E.O. of the Apollo Group, Inc., which owns the University of Phoenix. He is a billionaire.

Dr. Haller's research reminds us that just about anybody *can* overcome adversity and do something constructive. But most of us need a little help.

Perhaps the reason so many people struggle, and so many more give up all pretense of even struggling, is that not enough people walk into the marketplace and hold out a helping hand.

CHAPTER EIGHT

Where Are The True Priests?

T he true priest will benefit the most from this message. A true priest in our culture is often a very frustrated person. He sees the manipulation and controlling of the false priests around him, and he doesn't want to follow that model. He wants to see the sheep truly grow.

A Message to the True Priest

Seek out by way of the Holy Spirit the King or Kings to whom God has assigned you. Once the Lord reveals them to you, sit down and apply the principle of keeping quiet. Let the King talk. He will tell you in what areas he needs ministering. Seek out the Kings. Keep your heart pure without the motivation of money. That King is not the solution to your issues, for you still have other issues; but the King is part of the solution that God wants to bring to your attention.

A true priest does not have everything that the people need. He knows there are others around him to fulfill certain roles, and he welcomes their gifts. He has to break away from the model that is frustrating him, since that model urges him to keep on doing things the same way they have traditionally been done. He has to allow himself to do things differently. Then he has to get back to the number one thing he is supposed to be doing: directing the Master's sheep to their rightful place in the kingdom.

The priests come from accepting God's call. The priests-in-waiting are those who don't know they are called to be a priest. Where are they? You will find them in a few groups.

The first group is completely separated from the worship center, because the worship center did not welcome their priesthood. You will find these priests outside of the model of "churchy" Christianity, but still doing the work of the Lord. Since they are truly called, no worship center on earth will stop them. The work they are called to do is not in a worship center, for they are not pastors shepherding, but priests declaring "thus saith the Lord." You will find these true priests serving in places like YMCAs, Salvation Armies, Feed the Children, and so on, because their gifts are welcomed there.

The second group of priests is sitting in the marketplace. They are out of position and do not really fit in there. They do not want to be like the false priests they have seen, so they have migrated over to the area of a "pseudo-King." A pseudo-King enjoys feeding and equipping the people over the day-to-day operations of running a business. Sometimes, his business suffers for his focus is on working with the people. These priests are not great performers in the marketplace, but their hearts are pure.

Thirdly, you will find priests in gangs. The gangs are not just for pseudo-Kings, but they are also for misguided priests. I know two men who know the Word better than most pastors ever will. Yet, they are out sleeping around with women, selling dope and doing all kinds of worldly activities. When they are given the opportunity to be pulled aside to start talking about the Word, they show that they know it inside and out. They know the Word beyond what you will normally hear in a worship center, for their understanding of the Word is deeper than you can learn by only attending Sunday services. You will understand why they don't want to be in those worship centers that betray God's word. Unfortunately, they could not think of any alternative but the gangs, since they desire to be part of a family.

How do we reach the priests-in-waiting? How do we make sure these misguided priests not only know that God is calling, but also take them to a place where they have the courage to step out on the Lord's promises? The Lord has to speak into the hearts of His people to let them know where His priests are.

The King helps with this when he creates a kingdom that says, "We need you." A kingdom needs priests and places of worship. A true King will not hinder a budding priest from declaring what saith the Lord. But a false priest will. A King won't tell a priest to sit down with the excuse that "it isn't the priest's time." But a rival priest will.

The false priests are the ones killing the true priests. They are doing this intentionally. If a priest is extremely anointed, he is not going to be invited into too many worship centers. Why not? His true anointing exposes the false priest.

Priests kill one another with the burgeoning *"one church, multiple locations"* model. Some churches are even using holograms, where one pastor holograms himself into ten or twenty locations. Do these priests seriously mean to tell me that one person's revelation is so good and so strong that God does not want anybody else teaching at any of the other locations? This is a lie of the Devil.

This very model is sweeping through today's church. It leaves the people without a true shepherd and unequipped. The false priests have time to take up an offering, but no time to bring healing, deliverance and true freedom to the people.

It destroys the people, but it also destroys the priests-in-waiting who could have been put into one location to pastor a congregation. If the sheep had a real shepherd, they would understand why they did not need a hologram image of a preacher who takes their money—but is never present. The greedy priests would be out of a job. That is why they are deliberately pushing out the real priests-in-waiting.

It is just amazing how spiteful they can be. Pastor Sheppard, my friend, moved to the Raleigh, NC, area to plant a church. He reached out to other established pastors for friendship and guidance, only to be told that he was not welcome in the area, and he was bound to fail!

Being heartbroken, but not dismayed, Pastor Sheppard began to teach the Word in a small facility. He followed up his expositions with simple instruction on living in the Word. He loved the sheep and followed the instruction of his elders, who were local business leaders.

The neighboring pastors are constantly trying to disparage Pastor Sheppard's ministry. He isn't one of their "in-crowd," and he doesn't fit their stereotype of what a pastor "should" be. Fortunately, Pastor Sheppard does not measure his success by the size of the congregation but by the personal growth of the sheep. He keeps walking with the local Kings who have helped to increase his leadership ability as well as his effectiveness with the sheep. His sheep are growing in both stature and in numbers.

Less than three years later, Pastor Sheppard continues to gain in influence with the local Kings, while the other pastors continue to stare in amazement.

CHAPTER NINE
True Leadership

L eadership is one of the most misunderstood concepts in today's church. When a King is operating in true leadership, he is an **influencer**. His power is in his influence. When his influence is sent out properly, it yields his intended results. A King will, more than likely, operate behind closed doors and will not want many people around him on a daily basis. He can tell when the ones to whom he has delegated authority are doing what he says and accurately communicate it to the people, for he sees the people manifesting good fruit.

A King does not want to be set up on a pedestal by the people since, as a King, he has already been placed on a spiritual throne by God. Mere humans did not put him there. He knows that the way he is called to lead is through what comes out of his mouth in instruction and vision. If the people are struggling or failing, he will send for a man of God to make sure he is hearing the Lord rightly. Then he will get up and make sure that those to whom he delegated authority are doing their job. That is very critical for him.

A true leader is also looking for duplication. The real reflection of his leadership lies in whether or not he can look around and see himself in those he is leading. If he cannot, he knows there is a disconnect somewhere. [1]Myles Monroe gives a powerful definition of a King. He states that:

> *It is the governing influence of a King over a territory impacting it with his will, his purpose and his intent to produce a citizenry of people who reflect the King's morals and values.*

A true King-leader knows that the way he evaluates his leadership is to see if his constituents reflect his example, purpose and vision.

That is what Jesus did. As the Word says, "Let this mind that is in Christ be also in you" (see Philippians 2:5, NIV) and "Be ye transformed by the renewing of your mind" (Romans 12:2, NIV). A King knows the reason he is called and knows that he must get the citizenry to understand this. A true leader is leading you to a destination. He does not arrive overnight, and the product is a result of a process—discipleship.

---

1   Monroe, Myles. "Rediscovering The Kingdom." www. kingdomlifestyleministries.org/kingdomprinciples

[2]There are universal laws that come with leadership. John Maxwell speaks of these in his work, *The 21 Infallible Laws of Leadership*. In order to fulfill the King's purpose, intent, morals and values, he has to create an environment that grows people. One of the first ways to do this is by following these universal laws of leadership. Understanding these laws will correct the errors that have caused the chasm between Kings and priests.

The first law John Maxwell shares is the **Law of the Lid**. This law says that a King's leadership is like a lid over his organization or business. This lid operates like a ceiling. This is why a corporation or company that needs to be fixed removes the leader. A leader knows that people must grow or increase their lid or capacity. This does not come unless a follower is challenged and the leader gives him the space and responsibility to grow.

This is why a soldier cannot go from being a sergeant to being a general in the military. He has to pass through a process that increases capacity. He must go from being a corporal, a sergeant and then to a lieutenant to increase his capacity to lead. If at any point a King stops this growth, someone is showing him that the soldier cannot handle the next level of growth. A true leader is always looking for that point in which additional responsibility or authority is handled, so he knows where to draw the boundary.

---

2   Maxwell, John C. 2007. *The 21 Irrefutable Laws of Leadership: Follow Them and People Will Follow You.* Nashville, TN: Thomas Nelson.

The other law always at work for a leader is the **Law of Influence**. My mentor, Fred, taught me this law more from observation. He taught me that a leader is not determined by whose name or picture is on the wall of the building. A true leader's ways are shown through his followers.

I knew without a doubt when a dealership belonged to Fred. His dealerships had an unmistakable system. When you walked onto Fred's dealership, the cars were lined up in a particular way, the people were dressed a particular way, and the showrooms and bathrooms looked a certain way. You would know there was a standard of excellence in the place because this was Fred's way. A leader's influence is reflected in the people he leads.

A Leader Understands Process

When a leader understands the process of building capacity, emotional strength, vision and momentum in others, he understands process. He should not put a person in a position until he has been trained and the person is ready. The church is too quick to do the opposite, which is to put a friend or family member in a position even if the person is not ready. This undermines the process or timing of leadership.

One of the best business people in the world was Henry Ford, who developed a model of the assembly line for automobiles. This model was born out of his understanding that the less he gave people to focus on, the more effective they could be. He let them handle particular stations first, and if they proved that they could do that part well, then he let them move to another station. He did not allow anyone to lead or run his company without understanding each station.

When Ford was developing me to be a car dealership owner, I had to work at different positions within the company, some of which I did not like. One position that I hated was called Market Representation Department. It entailed contractual and legal processes for dealerships. Being a salesman with an entrepreneur's mind, I hated sitting in an office having to look at reports and contracts all day. Yet it was necessary because understanding that part of the process allowed me to excel years later.

A leader takes his citizens through developmental steps. He will not keep them stagnant. He will not brag about the fact that someone has been in a position ten, twenty or thirty years—unlike the current church model that allows bragging about the stagnation of people. A leader knows how to guide a constituent through this process and keep him growing to prepare him for the next level of authority. He empowers him to be fully equipped for the place to which God has called him. It has to happen correctly. If someone is placed too quickly, without proper equipping, then it can destroy him.

The **Law of Navigation** says that anyone can steer a ship, but it takes a leader to chart the course. A leader has an internal compass. This compass is his vision. When I teach a class, I always ask the question, "What does your vision look like?" If participants cannot answer this question, they cannot direct others.

Part of the Law of Navigation requires that you understand that the leader charts the course. A manager steers it, but a leader lays out the vision and directs arriving at the destination of success. He assigns managers to carry out the vision in stages and assigns roles so everyone arrive as a team. He receives the course that he needs to chart from the vision God gave him and knows how to recognize and place the gifts of the people.

When I walked into my first dealership, I had never worked in a parts department, service department or a collision center. I had worked as a General Sales Manager and was now apprehensive about being an owner. I felt my inexperience would disqualify me to direct every position. It did on some level, since I could not tell a technician how to change oil. Then the Lord dealt heavily with me about this and revealed that He had brought me through corporate steps and higher levels of retail to put me in a seat of ownership. The Lord did not need me to know how to do everybody else's job.

A leader places people into strategic management positions to empower them to share his instructions with the rest of the team in a language and style they will understand. For example, I spoke what I desired to the service director, and that service director took my instructions to the service technician in a language he could receive and understand. A leader understands that communication at the top level differs from communication at the bottom levels of the organization. That is why he desires to influence and delegate to the leadership he selects. If I were to share the vision of the company directly with the service technicians, it would have blown their minds. They would not have been able to see the vision, as the only thing they knew was that they were supposed to repair and restore vehicles. If I shared the direction in which I was taking the entire dealership, I would have lost them.

The **Law of Addition** simply says that leaders add value by serving others. John Maxwell states that great leaders nurture other great leaders below them. He explains that a selfish leader does not develop the leadership qualities in others. When he meets with his leadership team, the leader talks at the beginning and is then quiet. It is a sure sign of an immature leader when a team member talks incessantly. He evaluates the ones around him by what they are speaking and the results they are producing. This means that a team member cannot fool a leader by pretending to know something.

A leader loves it when his team not only sounds like him and knows what he knows, but when they learn it faster than he did. This is a true leadership model. They should grow faster if they are around you as a true leader. Paul instructed those he was teaching to learn his ways, as He learned the ways of Christ. If the leader is insecure, he will hinder the process and not want his team to grow beyond him. The greatest compliment true leaders can receive is for those whom they have developed to exceed them. When a businessman starts to grow older and become more legacy-minded, he will call people around to make sure that they acquire all of his knowledge and wisdom to continue his legacy. This is what Warren Buffet, one of the wealthiest businessmen in the world, does every year.

If a leader understands this, he will keep people around him to keep depositing into them, so they can learn faster then he learned. This is true discipleship. That is why Roy Williams is going to become the highest-winning basketball coach faster than Dean Smith did. Dean Smith became the number one winning coach in less time than Forest Phog Allen. And Forest Fog Allen did it faster than his predecessor, James Naysmith. These men were all disciples. The disciple should always exceed the one who disciples him.

When I was in the car dealership business, you met Fred when you met me. You met Fred's dealership operations when you came into my building because I was Fred's disciple. The closer the relationship I had with Fred, the more my business and how I operated reflected him, and the less you would see of him. People would quite possibly notice that I kept talking about this man whom they never saw, for although Fred was a person, he represented a way of thinking, a mindset and a way of doing things that produced results.

Leadership is a spiritual gift, but too many pastors kill the gifting of the up-and-coming Kings. This happens in the religious community as well as in the Black community. They kill the Kings early, since a

King's God-given vision makes him a dreamer. When Joseph received the dream, it was time to kill him, since his dream exposed the corruption of others. His dream included his lording over others, but his dream included vision. Joseph's brothers tried to kill him to prevent him from entering into what would one day be his position of overseeing for the King. A dream that is not being executed is only a dream. When it is executed, it is no longer a dream; it becomes a kingdom. False leaders know that if they can assassinate the dream early, it will never manifest throughout the land. This means the people who need it won't see it come to fruition.

The **Law of Magnetism** states that you are whom you attract. A leader attracts people like himself, and you can always tell who he really is by who is around him. A true leader knows that his aim is to get his team to walk beside him. He may start out in front, but he wants them beside him, and he eventually wants to be encouraging them from behind. That leader is still the leader, but he is operating in the way the Lord created true leadership.

If you are a true leader, everything about you gives those around you permission to be who they are. My mentor, Fred, had disciples who were in charge but still very connected to him. He didn't have a problem with putting his team out in front, since we were still under his umbrella. Everything about a true leader says there is no need to be like everybody else. It's good enough to be yourself. A real leader will never ask you to change your personality. He will never tell you to be docile when you are an aggressive person, or to be aggressive when you have a naturally gentle presentation. He will require you to mature and he will require you to operate in authority, but he will not tell you to change your personality.

If a leader tries to change your personality, you are working under the wrong person. A real leader knows that your authentic personality is needed. He sends an aggressive person out to accomplish something that needs aggression, and a gentle person to accomplish something that needs gentleness. A real leader selects you and tells you what he needs you to say on his behalf *in your own style*. If the client to whom he sent that aggressive emissary complains, "Your man was in my face!"—a true leader will think that is great because that was exactly what he sent him out to do. If the same leader on another day sends out a laid-back type, then a laid-back personality was needed to achieve his desired outcome at that time.

Pastors and True Leadership

I love Bill Hybels—pastor of Willow Creek in South Barrington, IL—more than any other pastor I have met. When I was exposed to Bill Hybels, I saw a priest who understands his role. There is nothing ostentatious about him. There is nothing saying, "Look at me." He understands that his power is in his influence. If a pastor is truly reflecting the Master, he becomes His mouthpiece, then he speaks less and allows the manifestation of His Word to speak for him.

When Job's sufferings ended, he said to the Lord, "Before I had heard of You, now I see You." (Job 42:5, NIV) This model works for shepherds. Unfortunately, today's sheep don't know God's voice, as their shepherds keep talking *at* them. In today's religious model, the pastors keep around them people who are like lap puppies. These lap puppy team members are very weak, but this gives him comfort. He never develops them to excel, for he wouldn't *want* them to do anything better than he can do it—that would damage his own dominance. His desire to be in control of everything drives him to work himself to death. It does not occur to him to train and equip the sheep, leave them to work and then inspect the work. If a pastor has people around him carrying his books and belongings, you know they are a bunch of insecure people who feed the pastor's ego. People who surround a true leader are not walking behind him but with him. When a leader is trying to rule over people, he will have those people walk behind him.

On my client surveys, people write that they love going to church, doing church stuff, serving the church and that they love serving their pastor. A sheep saying that he loves his shepherd is like a business person saying that he just loves his job and doesn't ever want to grow beyond their current job. Only an insecure leader likes that. A true leader will say, "What do you mean you don't want to grow? What do you mean you don't want to learn anything else?" If that pseudo-leader keeps you stagnant, then you will be in that same job forever, but it will never be a job of key position of input within that company.

A shepherd should be offended if his sheep say, "I just love my pastor" or "I love going to my church." That is almost like cursing at the shepherd. He should be thinking, "What do they mean by loving the building? Why do they love coming here? What's wrong with them?" Their shepherd should be absolutely offended to hear this. If he isn't, then he is lapping up their ego-stroking flattery.

Jesus expects the Body of Christ to do even greater things then He did while he was here upon the earth (John 14:12). Jesus' model was one of positioning and empowering. If a model is not of Jesus, then it is from the Devil. When this false model of self-aggrandizing leadership is demonstrated in the Body of Christ, those supposed leaders must be removed.

Vision vs. Instruction from God

God gives vision to Kings and revelation and instructions to pastors. The King is to communicate clearly and oversee the vision. Then he speaks to the people and declares that this is the vision of the Lord and moves in making that vision a reality. He then leaves the people to carry out the vision. If he remains, he will undermine their gifting.

Throughout this process, the King calls on the priest for clarity and instruction. He needs the priest to tell him what the Lord is saying concerning his direction. The King needs to know—through the priest—

what saith the Lord. I do not imply the King should not learn to hear directly from God by way of the Holy Spirit, but we all need counsel.

> *But the Lord said unto him, "Go thy way: for he is a chosen vessel unto Me, to bear My name before the Gentiles, and kings, and the children of Israel.* (Acts 9:15, KJV)

A King is the financier of the vision. He writes checks when he hears of good work being done in the kingdom. Part of his ministry is to allocate resources, which includes the gifts of the people.

God told David how He wanted His house built. He gave Him very clear instruction and told him not to deviate from that instruction. David did not have the right to make a single change to God's instruction. David could not say, "Well, maybe He didn't want gold right there. Let me put platinum there instead." It is not the King's business to re-interpret the instructions. What God instructs is clear and specific. God shows a King the vision and the people that He has assigned to that vision. He renews their minds so He can instruct them on how to manifest the vision.

When a pastor says the destiny of his sheep is tied to his vision, he is deceived from his very core. While it doesn't seem like an untrue statement, it is a deceptive spirit, and he cannot be communicating it for any other reason than to control the congregation.

God's vision is never about a building. If that pastor's vision is from God, then it will contain the

Kingdom assignments and gifts of the sheep to which he is assigned. God's vision always goes beyond the four walls of a building and beyond the use of facilities. God only gives vision to a pastor who carries a King's anointing. A pastor who does not carry the King's anointing makes the sheep believe they are not supposed to build that restaurant, own that business, or use their creativity out in the marketplace. He tells the sheep they are to use their gifts inside the walls of that building. This proves that what he is presenting is not vision at all. If he can convince you to buy into that deception, then you will try to run a business in the worship center and wonder why it's going broke. That pastor who is not a true King will attempt to change your vision to conform to his.

All that the pastor should have for a sheep is instruction. Instruction is only a piece of the vision.

When God gives you a vision, that vision is always much bigger than one individual, and it stretches that person beyond his immediate location. When God gives you a vision, that vision is what He sees and wants you to see. Your vision becomes more powerful when you long to see more of God and become like Moses to whom "God spoke face to face, as a man speaks to his friend" (Exodus 33:11, NIV). When God shows you His vision, He shows you His face, which is a preview of what is to come. He shows you what is already done in Heaven, but you have not arrived there yet. Your task is then to communicate your vision in a way that the people under you can understand, for they are to play a role in realizing that vision.

How is a pastor to give instruction? Often he does not know. The Holy Spirit gives him revelation and the Word of God, and he labors to teach sound doctrine. But he struggles with the application. Usually he lacks the life-experience to know the course the sheep must take to realize the vision. When he doesn't have the experience, he usually adds theatrical fluff to distract the people from the fact of his inexperience.

How can a priest instruct the sheep on what he doesn't know himself? Making sure the sheep know how to apply the revelation and instruction should be the natural progression of the shepherd. It begins with revelation. He is only a conduit or tool for the revelation, and he cannot take credit for what is not his. He shares the revelation, and the people should ask, "How? Where is the instruction and accountability for application?" That is when the priest should step back and empower someone else to teach. This is also the role of the elders and other members of the body. The priest should know the sheep well enough to know who is succeeding in a particular area.

For example, the Bible says, "Love your wife as Christ loved the Church." As a priest, the pastor is in line with his calling when he declares the Word, whether as a Scripture or a *rhema* word from God for a particular person or time. So he may tell the congregation, "Love your wife," or "Be a man of God to her." The priest then delegates to that successful brother, whose marriage was in shambles ten years ago and now has one of the best marriages ever seen, an opportunity to instruct the other sheep on how he learned to apply the Word to his marriage. After the other men glean from his teaching and elevate their marriages, then the pastor should call up another brother, perhaps the one whose five-year marriage has succeeded from the very beginning, to tell the sheep how he did it. The instruction should come from those who have been through the experience because they are the ones who know how to succeed in that area. The sheep who are qualified to carry the application to share with the other sheep are revealed during the intimacy of fellowship. If the pastor doesn't give the sheep the opportunity to teach their application, he is just talking.

A priest who preaches, "All you need is the Word and Jesus" is lacking. Jesus is all you need for salvation, but you need a great deal more help for effective living on earth. Someone has to teach a babe in Christ how to crawl. You don't teach crawling by telling a child who is too young to speak, "Just crawl! The Word says crawl!" You have a process of placing the child's limbs and encouraging him to move. In the same way, people need instruction from the elders. Those who have been walking in the faith a long time should be teaching the young ones how to live effectively.

This is the main ingredient missing in today's worship centers. The cluelessness of the church system is obvious from the lack of fruit in the sheep's lives. So, is this about ignorance? Does *nobody* know how to live? Or are the older ones deliberately withholding the practical teaching? In that case, they are being manipulative. Too many pastors can only dish out the kind of information that they have read in a book, heard in someone else's sermon, or googled online. It is real easy to mimic someone else's words. You just fly your helicopter to a conference, write down whatever the preacher says, then fly back to your worship center and speak like a parrot.

I've heard big-name pastors prove that they cannot give instruction. Then they claim they have vision? No, what they have—God willing—is revelation to declare what saith the Lord. This does not add up to true vision. They cannot have vision with no resources and no instruction. That is why they need to hustle their congregations for the resources and just piggy-back on what someone else built or what somebody else did. That is not vision—that is imitation. That is why they are building the same type of buildings or life centers. If one of them has a King's mindset and does something different, then all the rest will follow suit.

Leadership is Reflected in the State of the Physical Body

The state of a person's physical body is a direct reflection of where he is spiritually. It is much more closely related to leadership than you would think. Everyone influences other people. Whether it is your mom and dad, grandparents, neighbors, coworkers or politicians who influence you. They model behaviors and habits, and you copy them. If a pastor or King doesn't have self-control over his body, the most obvious area of his health that others can see, then what kind of example is he setting for his congregation? How can we be a witness to, help win anyone to Christ, or lead in the marketplace? This leader will create a lifestyle and culture of undisciplined people.

A leader is extra responsible in the area of his health and self-control because other people are watching him to model a particular way of living. When he shows a lack of self-control in his emotional maturity, his time-budget, his eating behavior or his spending, he is directly affecting the lives of those under his influence.

You simply have to love the Jesus of the Bible. I'm not talking about the weak, poor image of Jesus whom most Christians say they are following. I am talking about the bold, authoritative King Jesus of the Bible. As Jesus dealt with the hypocrisy of the Sadducees and the Pharisees, He would declare that they were blind and fools. You have to love the Jesus of the Bible for unapologetically leading and knowing who He is. He modeled a behavior of discipline and certainty.

Leadership is Not Emotionalism

I refuse to believe that Jesus was emotive and dramatic. He did not punctuate His teaching of the multitudes or the disciples with a "Hmmmm" or a "Haaauuuhhh" or a "Yu'all don't hearrrr me." Jesus is the embodiment of discipline and self-control, and He knows who He is. Anyone who adds to His Word is not truly representing Him. It is a great insult to claim that we are ministering the Word of God then adding emotionalism and a rhythm and a "Hmmmm" to excite the people. The Word of God stands on its own power. It can excite the spirit of people without the help of our additions.

The sheep of this emotional pastor are in hideous spiritual, physical and mental shape. They don't know any other way, when their pastor is entertaining the people instead of shepherding them. You can tell when this spirit is present by the rocking motion of the people. The constant shouting, talking, running and standing up while the message is being delivered are signs of this spirit. To escape that cycle and walk in the fullness of life that God intended, the sheep need to turn away from that pastor and follow the ways of Christ.

The elders, the pastors, evangelists, prophets, teachers and apostles are supposed to teach and equip the Body of Christ and be a gift to it from God. First, the Body does not worship the gift—it worships the Gift-Giver. Second, the elders are supposed to equip the sheep to send them out, out to their homes, their work environments and the marketplace to reflect the Kingdom of Heaven. Real leaders understand that their task is to create an environment where the sheep can grow, learn and thrive, so they can go out and fulfill their calling.

Leaders are to Hold People Accountable

If I assign someone to manage my business finances, then I have delegated the authority in the area of finances, but the responsibility is still mine. I must make sure the financial manager knows what is expected of him, and I must monitor him to hold him accountable to doing it daily. I don't micromanage. But having equipped the manager until I felt comfortable releasing that authority to him, I still inspect often.

We all need to be held accountable when we are battling areas of our lives that are not in line with God's ways and not aligned with His Kingdom. The first thing to do is find someone who operates in a particular authority from Christ and who walks in it, whether it is in the area of money, time, health or anything else. Then we must allow that person to teach and instruct us and hold us accountable for applying it.

Here is a sure sign that the structure of the modern "church" has strayed beyond recognition from God's blueprint in the Bible. Pastors are releasing a pile of information in the worship center, but they give no mandate for its application. When there is no mandate for application, no real application ever takes place. When teaching is applied, people are held accountable for applying it. That way it becomes a discipline within them, and it changes their old nature. They become new people with new ways of doing things. The teaching becomes a transformation. Perhaps a person reduces from 400 pounds to 150 pounds. Perhaps the debtor who scrounges from paycheck-to-paycheck begins to live in abundance. Marriages are saved and old enemies are reconciled. Whatever the transformation, it comes by way of guidance and instruction followed by application and accountability.

All of us need some transformation. If you are a married man, you lead your home, so transformation there begins with you. It must start with you evaluating the culture by which you are allowing your family to live. Is it spiteful? Is it disorderly? Is your family eating out all the time? Are you not managing your money properly? Are you not communicating a clear vision for the home with your spouse?

Leadership has to come from a visionary standpoint and take people further than they can take themselves. A leader with vision sees further ahead than other people can. A leader's vision can paint a picture of your destination. You just have to love the way Jesus told the disciples to follow Him. That meant that He knew He was heading somewhere.

Leaders Endure and Persist

I was recently in an exercise class with a new instructress. We were kicking, sweating and stretching as usual, but some of us were slowing down and seemed to want to quit. At times, I felt I just didn't want to give it my all, even though I usually enjoy the feeling of pushing myself. While we were working out, the instructress was going harder than all of us. I said to myself, "Wow,

she must really be in shape! She is crushing us today."
Then she turned to the other side to kick. Do you
know what I saw? This woman, who was burning me
out, was pregnant. I could barely believe my eyes. She
was about five months pregnant. My admiration for
her sky-rocketed. Not only had she been pushing us
hard from the very first minute, but she was doing it
under a "handicap." Her amazing example energized
me and inspired me to persist.

As a leader, I am very seldom around people who
will push and motivate me. However, a leader must
remain around people who energize him. Successful
leaders share certain traits. One of these is that they
have undergone many difficulties, yet they have never
given up. Some of them have gone bankrupt, but they
never quit. No matter what the challenge, successful
leaders have not quit. I like to say, "Winners are made
of failures who didn't quit." If we are honest with
ourselves, most of us quit everything we do. Most of us
are quitters, yet we try to obtain a godly result in this
quitting, lackadaisical, and mediocre mindset.

Affluence comes through discipline, consistency,
commitment, faithfulness and good stewardship. To
people who understand how much discipline is required
for success, it is offensive to suggest anything else.
Think of the greatest saint in your church, the person
who has withstood the storm and emerged stronger
and sweeter for it. What would you think of someone
who said, "I would like that person's anointing but,
of course, I don't want to suffer all of his hardships?"
What a person has suffered—the depth at which he

has experienced what God can do in his life—is what makes his anointing so strong. It is through his challenges that he has become intimate with the names of Jehovah: Jehovah-Jireh, Jehovah-Rapha, Jehovah-Nissi—as did the Israelites.

Getting Ourselves Right

The marketplace needs well-equipped people of God to produce work of an excellent standard and to manifest God's word to others.

You don't know what you can do until you enter environments where you have to overcome a difficulty. It's like mountain climbing. It might seem crazy that some people climb mountains, but the reason people climb mountains, with all its risks and hardships, is because they want to push themselves to discover just how much they are capable of doing. There are other groups of people who operate totally by fear. They don't want to do much of anything. They don't see the value in taking risks, being pushed, or pushing themselves to do anything whatsoever—especially things they don't think they can do.

It is really simple to understand. Before we can make any improvements to other people or our environment, we must honestly evaluate **ourselves**. This is only difficult in the sense that we might not be *willing* to do it. Christians can be some of the most hypersensitive people. They complain that you can't talk about them and their private issues, yet judgementalism is rampant within the Body of Christ. The condition of the land is tied into the condition of the believer. The Lord said:

> *If My people who are called by My name will humble themselves and fast and pray and turn from their wicked ways; then will I hear from Heaven, and will forgive their sin, and will heal their land.* (2 Chronicles 7:14, NIV)

We don't want to be challenged on the fullness of who we are. We are too quick to compartmentalize our lives. A man who claims to be a Christian might still completely lack discipline in his health habits, still scream at his wife, still cheat on his tax return, or get plastered on Friday nights. This same man might whistle on his way to church and assume that everything is all right, as long as he writes his tithe or offering check.

I want to see people built up. I want to see all Christians come into the knowledge of who Christ is and who they are in Him, and then go out and be laborers for Him. Our problem is we're not hearing from Kings who understand the authority that believers have in Christ and who then model that authority to the people. When this authority is modeled, believers can identify that they are children of this authoritative God and understand that they are joint heirs with this very powerful Jesus Christ. They understand that they have all rights and privileges of the Kingdom on a deeper level. Until that message is taught powerfully and effectively, people will continue to overeat, continue to buy cars and waste money on other frivolous, worldly items, continue to want more and more, and continue to die.

A Christian should represent the Kingdom and Christ in every area of his life. The Christ of the Bible says believers are to walk in His authority and are to know who they are in Him. 1 Corinthians 7 says that if a believer was a slave before, he is now the Lord's freeman. If he was a freeman before his conversion, he is now a slave to Christ. Christ brings you into His Kingdom and gives you a new identity. (see Romans 8:17).

Believers know the clichés, but they don't know how to walk in the power of Jesus. This tells me that the teaching that influences their minds is not from God. Believers of today can't pray over a cold, can't cast the devil out of a frog, and can't overcome the temptation to drink a can of soda because they have no foundation in the true Word of God. The sheep do have a lot of entertainment, a lot of big buildings, a lot of conferences, a lot of people with Bentleys, but they don't know who they are.

Traditional ways of thinking and acting are what have brought us to this dreadful condition. Our real battle is to overcome these traditional attitudes. I know there are some people who are still trying to make their money and create their power from talking about civil rights. But the real battle is not civil rights, it is getting ourselves right. I call it, "Getting me right." They will not change how we are training our children. They are not going to change how we think, how we constantly fuss at one another, how we don't mentor, how we don't become involved in our kids' schools, how we don't volunteer, or how we don't support one another. These matters are not about civil rights. They are about "Getting me right." What we need to work on is getting our minds right in Christ.

It starts with you and me. You can be the King of your home, office and neighborhood. It can start there. But first, you must be willing to look in the mirror to address, not civil rights, but getting *you* right.

CHAPTER TEN

Restoring the Order of the King and the Priest

"Thou art the man!" With these words, the prophet Nathan exposed David's sin in stealing another man's wife and murdering the man. King David responded to the prophet's words with repentance and faith (2 Samuel 12:7-13, NIV).

The relationship between a King and a priest is fulfilling, rewarding and necessary if both are to accomplish God's will in the land. We see it when Joseph and Pharaoh save Egypt from famine (Genesis 41:46-49). We see it when Daniel and Darius set up an effective infrastructure all over the Persian empire, and Daniel supervises the honesty of the local governors "that the King might not suffer loss" (Daniel 6:2, NIV). We see it when Ezra and Nehemiah, a godly priest walking with a godly King, build a wall to protect Jerusalem, but recognize the wall will be useless unless the citizens are also protected from internal corruption. So they set up a pledge to regulate marriage, commerce, the Sabbath and the Temple cult according to God's holiness.

Chillingly, we see it when the prophet Samuel walks with a King who has treated God's instructions with contempt. Unlike Pharaoh and Darius, who were pagans, Saul has had the opportunity to hear God's words all his life. He could have chosen to be like Nehemiah. Yet he repeatedly disobeys God and ignores multiple warnings from the priest whom God has placed at his side. Finally, the only remaining message that Samuel can bring him is:

> *"Because you have rejected the Word of the Lord, He has rejected you as King."* (1 Samuel 15:23, KJV).

Best of all, we see it in Jesus, who is both Priest and King, as He trains His disciples. Jesus kept the disciples on a marketplace or community focus. This models for us the principle that the information that a King receives from a priest should focus on how to apply God's words in the marketplace or kingdom. A priest who knows God's voice and His will and ways to a King is giving the King direction for his rule. A King needs a priest to interpret vision, to reveal dreams, to be confronted on his immoral decisions, to provide revelation and friendship.

The Bible explains through these stories and examples the walk that God has ordained for the priest and King. Both the King and the priest have very lonely positions and, in many cases, God requires isolation. As both establish very few relationships that are fulfilling to both sides, the King's relationship with the priest must be one of these fulfilling relationships.

A Word to Those who Lead Priests

Who is responsible for making sure the shepherds are submitted to the will of God and protecting the sheep? I recently asked a man whom I respect in the Body of Christ, "Who protects the sheep from a corrupt shepherd?" He replied that the bylaws and systems put in place in Biblical days ensured the sheep were not being misdirected. The letters from Paul to the churches addressed many issues, including sexual immorality. Many of the very problems he addressed are running rampant in today's worship centers (see 1 Corinthians 5).

My study took me to the early church, where elders and apostles were installed to provide oversight. With all of the people who call themselves bishops, apostles and overseers around the church, you would expect some oversight would be going on somewhere. We have already considered this key Scripture more than once, but it bears repeating.

Here is a trustworthy saying: Whoever aspires to be an overseer desires a noble task. Now the overseer is to be above reproach, faithful to his wife, temperate, self-controlled, respectable, hospitable, able to teach, not given to drunkenness, not violent but gentle, not quarrelsome, not a lover of money. He must manage his own family well and see that his children obey him, and he must do so in a manner worthy of full respect. (If anyone does not know how to manage his own family, how can he take care of God's church?) He must not be a recent convert, or he may become conceited and fall under the same judgment as the devil. He must also have a good reputation with outsiders, so that he will not fall into disgrace and into the devil's trap.

In the same way, deacons are to be worthy of respect, sincere, not indulging in much wine, and not pursuing dishonest gain. They must keep hold of the deep truths of the faith with a clear conscience. They must first be tested; and then if there is nothing against them, let them serve as deacons. In the same way, the women are to be worthy of respect, not malicious talkers but temperate and trustworthy in everything. A deacon must be faithful to his wife and must manage his children and his household well. Those who have served well gain an excellent standing and great assurance in their faith in Christ Jesus.

Although I hope to come to you soon, I am writing you these instructions so that, if I am delayed, you will know how people ought to conduct themselves in God's household, which is the church of the living God, the pillar and foundation of the truth. Beyond all question, the mystery from which true godliness springs is great:

> *He appeared in the flesh,*
> *was vindicated by the Spirit*
> *was seen by angels,*
> *was preached among the nations,*
> *was believed on in the world,*
> *was taken up in glory.*
> (1 Timothy 3:1-16, NIV)

See also what the apostles tell us in these complementary passages:

To the elders among you, I appeal as a fellow elder and a witness of Christ's sufferings who also will share in the glory to be revealed: Be shepherds of God's flock that is under your care, watching over them—not because you must, but because you are willing, as God wants you to be; not pursuing dishonest gain, but eager to serve; not lording it over those entrusted to you, but being examples to the flock. And when the Chief Shepherd appears, you will receive the crown of glory that will never fade away. (1 Peter 5:1-4, NIV)

From Miletus, Paul sent to Ephesus for the elders of the church... "Keep watch over yourselves and all the flock of which the Holy Spirit has made you overseers. Be shepherds of the church of God, which he bought with his own blood." (Acts 20:17,28, NIV)

Have confidence in your leaders and submit to their authority, because they keep watch over you as those who must give an account. Do this so that their work will be a joy, not a burden, for that would be of no benefit to you. (Hebrews 13:17, NIV)

The elders who direct the affairs of the church well are worthy of double honor, especially those whose work is preaching and teaching. (1 Timothy 5:17, NIV)

Where are these church leaders and apostles today? When a corrupt pastor can stand in front of the sheep without ever being challenged, someone is not doing his job.

Who suffers when that happens? The sheep are being sent out into the marketplace with next to no knowledge of their authority and role. The Gospel is not preached, and the world does not hear. This problem affects everyone. As Jeremiah warns us:

The Righteous Branch

"Woe to the shepherds who are destroying and scattering the sheep of My pasture!" declares the LORD. Therefore this is what the LORD, the God of Israel, says to the shepherds who tend my people: "Because you have scattered My flock and driven them away and have not bestowed care on them, I will bestow punishment on you for the evil you have done," declares the LORD. "I Myself will gather the remnant of my flock out of all the countries where I have driven them and will bring them back to their pasture, where they will be fruitful and increase in number. I will place shepherds over them who will tend them, and they will no longer be afraid or terrified, nor will any be missing," declares the LORD.

The days are coming, declares the LORD, when I will raise up to David a righteous Branch, a King who will reign wisely and do what is just and right in the land. In His days Judah will be saved, and Israel will live in safety. This is the name by which He will be called: The LORD Our Righteousness. So then, the days are coming," declares the LORD, "when people will no longer say, 'As surely as the LORD lives, who brought the Israelites up out of Egypt,' but they will say, 'As surely as the LORD lives, who brought the descendants

*of Israel up out of the land of the north and
out of all the countries where He had banished
them.' Then they will live in their own land.*
(Jeremiah 23:1–8, NIV)

Who is dealing with the many lies that pour out
of the mouths of some shepherds? My mentor told me
that no one is defending the sheep from the corrupt
pulpit. Those who know better are often silent out of
a desire not to rock the boat. I say, to heck with the
boat! Go out and protect the sheep! Listen to what
the Word says about lying prophets, as we continue in
Jeremiah 23:

*Concerning the prophets: My heart is broken
within me; all my bones tremble. I am like a
drunken man, like a man overcome by wine,
because of the LORD and his holy words.
"The land is full of adulterers; because of the
curse the land lies parched and the pastures
in the desert are withered. The prophets follow
an evil course and use their power unjustly.
Both prophet and priest are godless; even in
My temple I find their wickedness," declares
the LORD.*

*"Therefore their path will become slippery; they
will be banished to darkness and there they
will fall. I will bring disaster on them in the
year they are punished, declares the LORD.
Among the prophets of Samaria I saw this*

repulsive thing: They prophesied by Baal and led My people Israel astray.

"And among the prophets of Jerusalem I have seen something horrible: They commit adultery and live a lie. They strengthen the hands of evil-doers, so that no one turns from his wickedness. They are all like Sodom to Me; the people of Jerusalem are like Gomorrah. Therefore, this is what the LORD Almighty says concerning the prophets: "I will make them eat bitter food and drink poisoned water, because from the prophets of Jerusalem ungodliness has spread throughout the land."

This is what the LORD Almighty says: "Do not listen to what the prophets are prophesying to you; they fill you with false hopes. They speak visions from their own minds, not from the mouth of the LORD. They keep saying to those who despise Me, 'The LORD says: You will have peace.' And to all who follow the stubbornness of their hearts they say, 'No harm will come to you.'

"But which of them has stood in the council of the LORD to see or to hear His word? Who has listened and heard His word? See, the storm of the LORD will burst out in wrath, a whirlwind swirling down on the heads of the wicked. The anger of the LORD will not turn

back until He fully accomplishes the purposes of His heart. In days to come, you will understand it clearly.

"I did not send these prophets, yet they have run with their message; I did not speak to them, yet they have prophesied. But if they had stood in My council, they would have proclaimed My words to my people and would have turned them from their evil ways and from their evil deeds.

"Am I only a God nearby," declares the LORD, "and not a God far away? Can anyone hide in secret places so that I cannot see him?" declares the LORD. "Do not I fill Heaven and earth?" declares the LORD.

"I have heard what the prophets say who prophesy lies in My name. They say, 'I had a dream! I had a dream!' How long will this continue in the hearts of these lying prophets, who prophesy the delusions of their own minds? They think the dreams they tell one another will make My people forget My name, just as their fathers forgot My name through Baal worship. Let the prophet who has a dream tell his dream, but let the one who has My word speak it faithfully. For what has straw to do with grain?" declares the LORD. "Is not My word like fire," declares the LORD, "and like a hammer that breaks a rock in pieces?

"Therefore," declares the LORD, "I am against the prophets who steal from one another words supposedly from Me. Yes," declares the LORD, "I am against the prophets who wag their own tongues and yet declare, the LORD declares. Indeed, I am against those who prophesy false dreams," declares the LORD. "

"They tell them and lead My people astray with their reckless lies, yet I did not send or appoint them. They do not benefit these people in the least," declares the LORD.

False Oracles and False Prophets

"When these people, or a prophet or a priest, ask you, 'What is the oracle of the LORD?' say to them, 'What oracle? I will forsake you, declares the LORD.' If a prophet or a priest or anyone else claims, 'This is the oracle of the LORD,' I will punish that man and his household. This is what each of you keeps on saying to his friend or relative: 'What is the LORD's answer?' or 'What has the LORD spoken?' But you must not mention 'the oracle of the LORD' again, because every man's own word becomes his oracle, and so you distort the words of the living God, the LORD Almighty, our God. This is what you keep saying to a prophet: 'What is the LORD's answer to you?' or 'What has the LORD spoken?'

"Although you claim, 'This is the oracle of the LORD,' this is what the LORD says: You used the words, 'This is the oracle of the LORD,' even though I told you that you must not claim, 'This is the oracle of the LORD.' Therefore, I will surely forget you and cast you out of My presence along with the city I gave to you and your fathers. I will bring upon you everlasting disgrace—everlasting shame that will not be forgotten." (Jeremiah 23:9–38, NIV)

If the Church does not repent soon, removal is forthcoming. The true Apostles must rise up and defend the sheep from being slaughtered. We speak on sending our American troops into harm's way to protect the genocide of others—let's send in spiritual troops to stop the genocide of the sheep. I must tell you that if you choose to call it something other than genocide, you will do as America has done throughout history—ignore it until it is too late to save the multitudes who will be destroyed.

I think of Idi Amin, President of Uganda, being allowed to tyrannize his nation without any intervention. Early in Idi Amin's rule of terror, he was supported by the U.K., Israel and South Africa. They withdrew that support when they became aware of how he was slaughtering his people. His friends continued to include Libya, Russia and East Germany. They did not necessarily agree with every aspect of his politics. What they approved was the way the alliance channeled money into their hands. By the time Britain and other countries stirred themselves to intervene in Ugandan affairs, more than 300,000 people had been murdered.

Believers must not continue to sit on the sidelines and act as if destruction is not happening in the worship center. You are part of the Body of Christ, and all of us are connected by the Father through the Son and are joint heirs. You have blood on your hands if your priority is "not rocking the boat." I wonder how many of you are not speaking out because it will affect the money coming into your house. You hear and see the slaughter of the sheep. Will you come and fight for Christ?

The Biblical Process for Restoring Order among Priests

In the section on the role of the pastor, I have included a section of an [1]article by Craig Bluemel. The article continues to share how the Church is to bring scripturally-based order back into full operation. God did provide a clear process. And again, excerpts from Craig Bluemel's writing, which are based on the Word, say it better than I could. The article continues:

> **1 Timothy 5:20.** *Those (elders) who continue in sin, rebuke in the presence of all, so that the rest also may be fearful of sinning.*

---

1 Bluemel, Craig. "What is the biblical role of a pastor in a church?" http://www.bibleanswerstand.org/pastors.htm

---

1 Timothy 5:22. *Do not lay hands on anyone too hastily and thus share responsibility for the sins of others; keep yourself free from sin.*

Elders are to watch out for one another's lives and teaching. Here are some points to consider:

- A formal accusation against an elder brought before a tribunal of elders should not be received unless there are 2 or 3 witnesses.

- Such accusations are to be formal in nature (which would exclude hearsay or gossip) and must be fairly weighed before a board of elders.

- Discipline for an elder who continues in unrepentant sin is harsh because of his position and influence as a leader in the church.

When an elder is found guilty, the rebuke given to him before all is one by which he has been tried and convicted. 1 Timothy 5:21 (NIV) summarizes the attitude that is to be maintained by other elders when dealing with an accusation of sin in the eldership. The New International Version states, "... keep these instructions without partiality, and do nothing out of favoritism."

James 5:14. *Is anyone among you sick? Let him call for the elders [plural] of the church, and let them pray over him.*

This verse is consistent with all previously mentioned texts showing a group of elders being called upon to minister to the church in healing. It nowhere mentions having one pastor being called upon for such a ministry.

1 Timothy 3:1-7. *It is a trustworthy statement; if any man aspires to the office of an overseer it is a fine work he desires to do. An overseer, then, must be above reproach, the husband of one wife, temperate, prudent, respectable, hospitable, able to teach, not addicted to wine or pugnacious, but gentle, uncontentious, free from the love of money. He must be one who manages his own household well, keeping his children under control with all dignity (but if a many does not know how to manage his own household, how will he take care of the church of God?); and not a new convert, lest he become conceited and fall into condemnation incurred by the devil. He must have a good reputation to those outside the church, so that he may not fall into reproach and the snare of the devil.*

It is clear that leadership in our churches needs to be re-aligned to conform to the Biblical pattern. This change will not come easily, because it will call for a break with the tradition we have lived with for hundreds of years. Yes, God will continue to operate within the churches the way they are currently structured, but ultimately this will change as the church returns to the authority of Scripture over tradition.

Ephesians 4:11–13. *And He gave some, on the one hand, as apostles, and on the other hand, as prophets, and still again some as bringers of good news, (evangelists), and finally, some as pastors (shepherds) who are also teachers, for the equipping of the saints for ministering work with a view to the building up of the Body of Christ, until we all attain to the unity of the faith and of the experiential, full, and precise knowledge of the son of God, to a spiritually mature man, to the measure of the stature of the fullness of the Christ.* (From Wuest's Expanded Translation of the New Testament)

The offices of the church must be restored in their scriptural settings. In closing, let us carefully take to heart the words of Ezekiel the prophet, who warns the shepherds of Yahweh's judgment if ever they use force and severity to dominate the flock:

Ezekiel 34:1-4, 7-16a, 23-24, 29-31. *Then the word of the LORD came to me saying, "Son of man, prophesy against the shepherds of Israel. Prophesy and say to those shepherds, 'Thus says the Lord GOD, Woe, shepherds of Israel who have been feeding themselves! Should not the shepherds feed the flock? You eat the fat and clothe yourselves with the wool, you slaughter the fat sheep without feeding the flock. Those who are sickly you have not strengthened, the diseased you have not healed, the broken you have not bound up, the scattered you have not brought back, nor have you sought for the lost; but with force and with severity you have dominated them...*

"'Therefore, you shepherds, hear the word of the LORD: As I live, declares the Lord GOD, surely because My flock has become a prey, My flock has even become food for all the beasts of the field for lack of a shepherd, and My shepherds did not search for My flock, but rather the shepherds fed themselves and did not feed My flock; therefore, you shepherds, hear the word of the LORD: 'Thus says the Lord GOD, "Behold, I am against the shepherds, and I will demand My sheep from them and make them cease from feeding sheep. So the shepherds will not feed themselves anymore, but I will deliver My flock from their mouth, so that they will not be food for them.'

"For thus says the Lord GOD, 'Behold, I Myself will search for My sheep and seek them out. As a shepherd cares for his herd in the day when he is among his scattered sheep, so I will care for My sheep and will deliver them from all the places to which they were scattered on a cloudy and gloomy day. I will bring them out from the peoples and gather them from the countries and bring them to their own land; and I will feed them on the mountains of Israel, by the streams, and in all the inhabited places of the land. I will feed them in a good pasture, and their grazing ground will be on the mountain heights of Israel. There they will lie down on good grazing ground and feed in rich pasture on the mountains of Israel. I will feed My flock and I will lead them to rest,' declares the Lord GOD.

"'I will seek the lost, bring back the scattered, bind up the broken and strengthen the sick... Then I will set over them one shepherd, My servant David, and He will feed them; He will feed them Himself and be their Shepherd. And I, the LORD, will be their God, and My servant David will be Prince among them; I the LORD have spoken... I will establish for them a renowned planting place, and they will not again be victims of famine in the land, and they will not endure the insults of the nations anymore. Then they will know that

I, the LORD their God, am with them, and that they, the house of Israel, are My people,' declares the Lord GOD. 'As for you, My sheep, the sheep of My pasture, you are men, and I am your God,' declares the Lord GOD." (NASU)

SELAH... PAUSE, REFLECT & ALLOW GOD TO CHANGE YOUR HEART.

CLOSING

I n closing, I beg that you hear my heart. It is not my desire to undermine the importance of the order of the leadership in the Body of Christ, although, I have become frustrated by this misalignment of God's order. As a marketplace King who desires to see the full manifestation of the unity in the Body of Christ, I must do my assignment and yell to us all to put ourselves in order the way the Father intended.

I challenge you to consider this work as a call to all of us to be about the Father's business in the market-place and the worship centers. We can begin by asking ourselves: *Am I acting for myself or for the Kingdom? What would the harvest be if Kings and priests walked together like Samuel with David, and Nebuchadnezzar with Daniel?*

As I observe the condition of the Body of Christ, I see that we are in major need of spiritual surgery to remove the egos, pride, greed, racism and many other sins that have engulfed us in so many ways in our lives.

Pastors and Elders: Ask God to reveal the Kings in your area whom He has assigned to you to love, counsel, learn from and befriend. Go to these Kings with a heart to see God use their influence and resources to bless the people and align their kingdoms under Him.

Kings: Recognize the need for godly counsel, and that elders and pastors are gifts to us. As Kings, our role is critical to the land and it affects millions of people. We need a voice that declares what saith the Lord in the midst of all the voices. You can easily help the pastor and elders by meeting their basic financial needs while you are growing your Kingdom for God.

To my African-American friends everywhere: Please wake up and break away from the slavery of control and manipulation. The days are short, and your community has lost too many Kings. If we will not change—it may soon be too late. Create schools that are solely for Kings, and allow God to use them to build a kingdom for all people. It is time for God's true Kings to rise.

Warning to Kings

Do not make the mistake as Nebuchadnezzar by thinking you have accomplished any success on your own. Your talents and gifts are from God, and He deserves all the glory. This trap of worldly success has caused many, including myself, to become prideful, and it will result in a wilderness period until we see ourselves as sinners who are saved by the blood of Jesus Christ. Our role in the land should be welcomed with fear and reverence for God, the Father. I reference

Ecclesiastes 2 as a reminder that all personal success is vanity. We are only vessels created for His purpose.

As Kings, it is our nature to fight, and our battlefield is the marketplace. We are not put here for bible studies and to fund worship centers alone. We are called to be vessels to usher in the Kingdom of God in the territory assigned to us. Remember, the product is the Kingdom of God, and we are simple Kingdom Franchises given permission to use His name.

I challenge you to allow the Father to use you to unify the body of Christ in your land. Work with other righteous Kings by helping one another grow in the fullness of the stature of Christ. You are called to restore families, teach principles, fund ideas and prepare the body for the upcoming persecution. Use your television deals to promote Kingdom living…your influence to protect the sheep from the wolves in our land. Do you hear the cry of the widow, the single mom, the orphan, the poor, the fatherless, the hungry and those who are in religious bondage? They are crying out for Kings to arise. Will you answer the call?

ABOUT THE AUTHOR

Joel C. Wiggins understands that we are all empowered to represent the Kingdom of God to the world. Throughout his life, he has placed himself in position to see the lives of men and women positively affected by his witness. He considers it an honor and a privilege to serve as a mentor, counselor and friend to people all over the world.

Joel was born and raised in Kinston, NC. He is a proud graduate of North Carolina A&T University in Greensboro, NC. Upon graduation from college, Joel began a corporate career with Ford Motor Company. After several successful years with the company, his true spirit emerged, leading him to a life of entrepreneurship. Joel has owned several Ford and GM automotive dealerships, a collision center, and currently operates a host of enterprises, including custom clothing, real estate and a management firm.

Joel's true passion is discipleship. He recognizes that the only way truly to impact lives is to put all the cards on the table and just be "real." His transparency has inspired a men's group that meets weekly to discuss the principles of "being men." Additionally, Joel hosts a daily radio show, *The Empowerment Hour with Joel Wiggins*, designed to equip people to pursue greatness in every aspect of life. Joel has developed *John David Man*, which focuses on teaching entrepreneurship and leadership to young men. Joel also enjoys speaking to young men and women and encouraging them to achieve in life the way we all should – in excellence.

Joel's desire to make an impact in the community has resulted in several "movements," from *Get On The Bus* in 2006 to an annual Father-Daughter Dance, *Men & Boys Outing* in 2008, *Mother-Son Dance*, Family Empowerment conferences and a Mentoring Mansion program, which all focus on the importance of operating as a family. The Father-Daughter dance is especially close to his heart, as its mission is to ensure that as many girls as possible understand the strength of a father's love and attentiveness.

Joel's passion for marketplace leaders has led to the creation of many business mentoring programs: the *Kingmaker Series* for entrepreneurs; *Thugs to Kings* program for gang members and prisoners; and *Young Entrepreneurs* for kids ages 8 – 18. The programs teach the importance of ownership and leading and serving others through your gifts, talents and resources. The motivation behind this model is that ideas and treasures placed in people must be revealed and developed with a Kingdom of God perspective.

Joel serves on the Board of Directors for numerous organizations. He is a highly sought after speaker and workshop facilitator. He teaches others his mantra: "Know who He is, know who you are, GO!"

God has blessed Joel with a wife, a son and two daughters. He is a follower of Jesus Christ as his Lord and Savior and strives daily to be the ambassador of the Kingdom of God in this world.

CPSIA information can be obtained
at www.ICGtesting.com
Printed in the USA
LVOW11*1400270117

522410LV00006B/52/P